best of the best

Editor in Chief **Judith Hill**
Art Director **Elizabeth Rendfleisch**
Managing Editor **Miriam Harris**
Senior Food Editor **Dana Speers**
Assistant Editor and Designer **Colleen McKinney**
Wine Editor **Jean Reilly**
Production Coordinator **Stuart Handelman**

Senior Vice President, Chief Marketing Officer **Mark V. Stanich**
Vice President, Branded Products **Bruce Rosner**
Director, Branded Services and Retail Sales **Marshall A. Corey**
Operations Manager **Phil Black**
Business Manager **Doreen Camardi**

ISBN: 0-916103-74-9   ISSN: 1524-2862

FOOD & WINE

annual cookbook-awards collection

best of the best

The Best Recipes from the 25 Best Cookbooks of the Year

American Express Publishing Corporation
New York

FOOD & WINE
BOOKS

contents

desserts

introduction

Every time we undertake the task of choosing the best original, hardback cookbooks of the year and the best recipes from those books, we do so with pleasure. For months we get to look at, read, and test cookbooks. Are we disappointed when highly touted books don't deliver? Sure. But then there are those that make no big claims for themselves and turn out to be gems. Are we frustrated when recipes don't work? Definitely. But then there are those that not only work but surprise and delight. And in the end, when we have the top 25 cookbooks identified and the brilliant best recipes pinpointed—and can put them all in one book—our satisfaction and pride are sinfully strong.

In this, our fifth volume of *Best of the Best*, we continue the tradition of presenting the recipes as their authors recorded them. If the ingredient list was divided into sections, it is in this book as well; if the steps were numbered, they are here too; if there were hints, we've included them. Each recipe accurately reflects the book it comes from.

We've also let you know, in tips running along the bottom of the pages, our experiences while testing the recipes. You'll find our wine recommendations in the same place, unless the recipe already includes a beverage suggestion. We hope the tips and recommendations will be helpful to you. We *know* that you're in for some good eating when you make any recipe from this collection.

Judith Hill

Judith Hill, Editor in Chief
FOOD & WINE Books

editor's choice awards

Each year we agonize over choosing our very favorite books and recipes from an already hand-culled group. Here are our fifth annual Editor's Choice Awards—the best of the best of the best!

best cookbook of the year

Nuts: Sweet and Savory Recipes from Diamond of California
by Tina Salter
published by Ten Speed Press

best cookbook of the year: runner-up

Second Helpings from Union Square Cafe
by Danny Meyer and Michael Romano
published by HarperCollins Publishers

best recipe of the year: savory

Ecuadorian Potato-Cheese Soup with Avocado
from *Home Cooking Around the World: A Recipe Collection* by David Ricketts, page 44
published by Stewart, Tabori & Chang

best recipe of the year: sweet

Hazelnut Chocolate Meringue with Blackberries
from *A Year in Chocolate: Four Seasons of Unforgettable Desserts*
by Alice Medrich, page 226
published by Warner Books

prettiest book of the year

A Year in Chocolate: Four Seasons of Unforgettable Desserts
by Alice Medrich
published by Warner Books

roll call of winners—and why we chose them

The 25 best cookbooks of the year are listed here in alphabetical order, NOT by merit. Deciding on the sequence for a top to bottom roster would be a difficult task indeed since—as you can tell by our reasons for choosing the books—they're all exceptional.

1 **The Baker's Dozen Cookbook** *Become a Better Baker with 135 Foolproof Recipes and Tried-and-True Techniques* edited by Rick Rodgers
Favorite recipes from thirteen of the best bakers in the country—how can this book miss? Introductory pages, which begin the book and each chapter, amount to an informed and concise course on baking. Copious professional tips spread throughout the book are icing on the cake.

2 **BayWolf Restaurant Cookbook** by Michael Wild and Lauren Lyle
If Alice Waters, with her Chez Panisse, is the mother of Mediterranean-accented California cuisine, Michael Wild, the owner of BayWolf, could well be nominated as the father. A delicious portrait of this important restaurant.

3 **La Bella Cucina** *How to Cook, Eat, and Live Like an Italian* by Viana La Place
Bona fide Italian recipes that you haven't seen a million times. You're certain to find plenty here that has the magic combination: homey comfort provided by traditional food and excitement lent by the new-to-you.

4 **Biba's Taste of Italy** *Recipes from the Homes, Trattorie and Restaurants of Emilia-Romagna* by Biba Caggiano
Entirely authentic recipes from our favorite region of Italy. This book is packed with the simple yet sublime combinations that abound in real Italian cooking.

5 **Bobby Flay Cooks American** *Great Regional Recipes with Sizzling New Flavors* by Bobby Flay
A popular chef cavorts from New England to California (with a long stop in the Deep South) applying his own brand of flavor fireworks to all-American favorites.

One of America's most creative chefs discloses how and why he combines ingredients as he does. Large, close-up photos show exactly how the dish should look—and make you want to lick the page.

Here's a chance to enjoy the same dishes that the likes of Paul McCartney and Gwyneth Paltrow order at Da Silvano restaurant. Lots of photos of the place, its denizens, and its food make cooking from the book almost like being there.

There's no question—Chef Kunz is wildly inventive. You may wonder about some of his recipes (pork with a topping of salami, cornichons, and figs, page 71, for instance), but one taste will make you a convert. Glorious photos too.

An appealing little book whose title says it all: the recipes are for the kind of delicious, simple food you expect to get in an Italian wine bar. Excellent wine recommendations are provided by the author's son, Evan, a master sommelier.

Definitely old-fashioned, and we mean that in a good way. The recipes are down-home simple and down-home tasty—the kind that make everyone say *mmmmm.*

Ramsay is at present the only chef in England honored with three stars, the top Michelin rating, and this book shows why. Many clever riffs on classic—mainly French—pastries and other desserts.

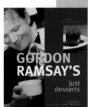

12 **Home Cooking Around the World** *A Recipe Collection* by David Ricketts
Easy favorites from a multitude of countries. None of the recipes require recherché ingredients or arcane methods. Lots of familiar dishes, but many delectable surprises as well.

13 **Italian Holiday Cooking** *A Collection of 150 Treasured Recipes*
by Michele Scicolone
Holiday, shmoliday. These recipes are good all year. In fact the collection is not limited to Christmas treats at all but includes dishes traditionally served on special days spread throughout the calendar. Most of the recipes are simple enough for any old day.

14 **Joanne Weir's More Cooking in the Wine Country** by Joanne Weir
The fine TV series *Weir Cooking in the Wine Country II* comes to your kitchen bringing recipes that are right in step with what home cooks want today. Fresh ingredients used in simple, straightforward dishes that draw inspiration from all over, but mostly from Italy and France.

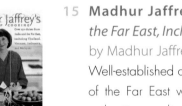

15 **Madhur Jaffrey's Step-by-Step Cooking** *Over 150 Dishes from India and the Far East, Including Thailand, Vietnam, Indonesia, and Malaysia*
by Madhur Jaffrey
Well-established as a superb Indian-cookbook author, Jaffrey applies herself to the cuisines of the Far East with equally enlightening results. The carefully chosen recipes give an authentic sampling, yet they're easy to make at home and appeal to Western tastes.

16 **The Naked Chef Takes Off** by Jamie Oliver
Every Jamie Oliver fan will want this one. He writes just like he talks on TV: he's chatty, he's fun, he's the antithesis of pomposity. All this and he can cook too.

17 **Napa Stories** *Profiles, Reflections & Recipes from the Napa Valley*
by Michael Chiarello
Three books in one: an interesting book about people who have made California wine country so successful, a beautiful book for your coffee table, and a cookbook with fantastic recipes from a great chef.

18 **A New Way to Cook** by Sally Schneider
Alchemist at work: Sally Schneider makes delicious food that's low in fat and calories. Many people try; few succeed. In addition, the more than 600 recipes in this book are meticulously tested and thoroughly explained. Clearly a labor of love.

19 Nuts *Sweet and Savory Recipes from Diamond of California* by Tina Salter

Yes, this cookbook was conceived by a company that markets nuts. But, no, it doesn't matter. The recipes were especially carefully thought through, developed, tested, and written. That at least a few nuts are used in every recipe is actually beside the point for the cook. From appetizers to desserts, each dish is a winner. Good photos too.

20 One Potato, Two Potato *300 Recipes from Simple to Elegant—Appetizers, Main Dishes, Side Dishes, and More* by Roy Finamore

Almost 600 pages of potato recipes? You bet! Every one is a gem. We think you'll find each of the basic recipes to be the best one you've ever tried for that dish—and you'll love the delectable new ideas as well.

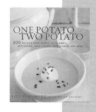

21 Pleasures of the Vietnamese Table *Recipes and Reminiscences from Vietnam's Best Market Kitchens, Street Cafés, and Home Cooks* by Mai Pham

The real deal—but without a plethora of impossible-to-find ingredients. The primarily simple recipes in this book make an excellent introduction to Vietnamese cooking.

22 Prime Time Emeril *More TV Dinners from America's Favorite Chef* by Emeril Lagasse

Well, it's Emeril after all. Who wants to miss the fun? Besides, there are lots of yummy, homey recipes here, along with some fancier ones. And he scatters a generous helping of tips—written in his own inimitable style—throughout the book.

23 Second Helpings from Union Square Cafe *140 New Favorites from New York's Acclaimed Restaurant* by Danny Meyer and Michael Romano

Union Square Cafe has been at the top of the Most Popular list in the Zagat Survey for five years. Cooking from this book will convince you that the restaurant deserves its kudos. And you don't even have to struggle for reservations.

24 Soffritto *Tradition and Innovation in Tuscan Cooking* by Benedetta Vitali

Genuine Tuscan. Recipes from an Italian chef who's owned a restaurant in Florence for two decades. The recipes here are exceptionally well tested and thoroughly explained.

25 A Year in Chocolate *Four Seasons of Unforgettable Desserts* by Alice Medrich

A must-have for the chocolate obsessed. You can keep yourself happy by making one recipe a week all year long. The desserts range from easy to elaborate, but most are at the simple end of the spectrum. And nearly all have tempting full-page photos.

hors d'oeuvres
& first courses

Nuts

crostini with cambozola, caramelized onions, and walnuts from NUTS

yields 24 crostini | The next time you're reaching for a box of crackers in the grocery store, put it back and pick up a baguette. Crostini, thin slices of bread crisped in the oven, are an easy homemade alternative to crackers; they are somehow both rustic and sophisticated—especially when you top them with sweet caramelized onions, toasted walnuts, and that creamy blend of Camembert and Gorgonzola called Cambozola.

$^1/_2$ cup chopped walnuts

24   slices baguette, cut $^1/_4$ to $^3/_8$ inch thick

$4^1/_2$ tablespoons extra-virgin olive oil

2   large red onions (about 1 pound total), thinly sliced

2   tablespoons chopped fresh sage

1   teaspoon balsamic vinegar

$^1/_4$ teaspoon salt

$^1/_8$ teaspoon sugar

Freshly ground pepper

4   ounces Cambozola, Bavarian blue, or other soft-ripe blue cheese,
      at room temperature

Preheat oven to 350°. Spread walnuts on a baking sheet or in a shallow pan. Bake, stirring once or twice, until lightly browned and fragrant, 8 to 10 minutes. Let cool.

Increase oven temperature to 400°. Arrange bread slices on a baking sheet; brush tops with 3 tablespoons of the oil. Bake until lightly toasted and golden brown, 5 to 7 minutes. Let cool. (If making in advance, store airtight.)

FOOD & WINE test-kitchen tips

- Use a food processor fitted with the slicing blade for weep-free onion cutting.

- If you can't find fresh sage, substitute 2 teaspoons dried crumbled leaves or $1^1/_2$ teaspoons ground (rubbed) sage.

In a large, heavy saucepan or flameproof casserole, heat the remaining 1 ½ tablespoons oil over medium heat. Stir in onions, sage, vinegar, salt, and sugar. Cover and cook, stirring occasionally, until onions are very tender and browned at the edges, 20 to 25 minutes. Season to taste with pepper. Stir in walnuts.

Spread each crostini with about 1 teaspoon cheese; then mound onion-walnut mixture on top. Serve slightly warm or at room temperature.

little mushroom tarts

from BAYWOLF RESTAURANT COOKBOOK

makes 12 tarts | Prepare these tarts as part of an appetizer platter. They reheat well the same day they are prepared, but not beyond that. If you need a million of them, assemble them the day before, then bake them the day you need them.

mushroom filling

4   ounces shiitake mushrooms, diced

8   ounces domestic mushrooms, diced

3   tablespoons butter

2   tablespoons olive oil

Salt and freshly ground black pepper

1   small onion, minced

2   garlic cloves, minced

Sherry vinegar to taste

2   teaspoons chopped Italian parsley

savory tart dough

6   tablespoons butter

1   cup all-purpose flour

Pinch of salt

$1/4$ cup plus 1 to 2 tablespoons cold water

Egg wash of 1 egg and pinch of salt

to prepare the filling Cook the mushrooms separately in a mixture of a scant spoonful each of butter and olive oil. Cook the shiitakes over medium-high heat until just browned, and then remove from the heat. Start the domestic mushrooms over high heat so they will release and reabsorb their juices, then lower the heat and cook slowly until they are dark brown and intense. Season the mushrooms well. Cool briefly. Chop finely. In one of the mushroom pans, caramelize the onion in 1 tablespoon of the butter. Just before removing the pan from the heat, add the garlic and deglaze the pan with the vinegar. Add the parsley and mix in the mushrooms. Adjust the seasoning; the mushrooms should be slightly salty and acidic so that they will be able to stand up to the pastry. Refrigerate. The tarts are much simpler to assemble if the filling is cold.

to prepare the dough Place the flour on a cutting board. Dice the butter into cubes and sprinkle it over the flour with the salt. Chop finely with a knife, as you would parsley, but make sure that the butter is not completely obliterated. We want little chunks here and there. Pour some of the water over it and gently push the dough with the heel of your hand. Use just enough water to bring the dough together, then wrap tightly in plastic and refrigerate for 15 to 20 minutes.

to assemble the tarts Roll the dough out thinly on a floured surface to a ¼- to ⅛-inch thickness. Brush half the dough with egg wash. Form the mushroom filling into 12 little balls, and line them up 1 inch apart on the egg-washed side of the dough, as though you were assembling ravioli. Fold the vacant side of the dough over the rows of filling, and gently press down around each mushroom mound. Make sure there is a good seal. Use a round or scalloped cookie cutter to cut out the tarts. The tarts can be prepared ahead to this point and refrigerated, covered with plastic wrap.

Bake in a preheated 375° to 400° oven for 15 to 20 minutes. The last 5 minutes of cooking, brush again with egg wash. The tops of the tarts should be golden brown. Serve warm.

FOOD & WINE test-kitchen tips

- Vary the flavor with a different herb if you like. Sage or tarragon would be nice.

- If you combine the ingredients for this lovely, flaky dough on a board (the chef's way), a plastic or metal dough scraper will greatly facilitate the process. Or, if it seems easier, you can put the flour and salt in a bowl, incorporate the butter with a pastry cutter, toss in the water with a fork, and press the dough into a ball.

spicy chicken-walnut triangles **from NUTS** | yields 36 triangles

These golden pastry triangles stuffed with a sweet-savory Moroccan-style chicken filling look and taste quite professional. They take a fair amount of time to make, but you can do all the preparation in stages and keep the unbaked triangles in the refrigerator or freezer until you're ready to serve them. (For storage, freeze them on baking sheets, then transfer them to plastic freezer bags. Frozen triangles can go straight from the freezer to the oven; add a few minutes to the baking time, and test the filling to be sure it's heated through.)

$^1\!/_2$ cup chopped walnuts

$1^1\!/_2$ tablespoons walnut oil or vegetable oil

$^1\!/_2$ cup finely chopped onion

1   skinless, boneless chicken breast half (about 6 ounces), finely chopped

2   tablespoons sweetened dried cranberries or raisins

1   tablespoon finely chopped pimiento-stuffed green olives

2   teaspoons mashed canned chipotle chiles in adobo sauce,
     or $^1\!/_2$ teaspoon crushed dried red chiles

1   small clove garlic, pressed or chopped

About $^1\!/_4$ teaspoon salt

$^1\!/_2$ teaspoon ground cumin

$^1\!/_4$ teaspoon ground cinnamon

$^1\!/_8$ teaspoon cayenne pepper

$^1\!/_2$ cup (about 2 ounces) shredded Monterey jack cheese

6   sheets filo dough, thawed

$^1\!/_2$ cup unsalted butter, melted

Preheat oven to 350°. Spread walnuts on a baking sheet or in a shallow pan. Bake, stirring once or twice, until lightly browned and fragrant, 8 to 10 minutes. Let cool.

In a medium frying pan, heat oil over medium heat. Add onion and cook until softened but not browned, about 5 minutes. Stir in chicken, cranberries, olives, chiles, garlic, salt, cumin, cinnamon, and cayenne. Cook, stirring often, until chicken is no longer pink, about 5 minutes. Taste and add salt if needed. Let cool. Stir in walnuts and cheese.

FOOD & WINE test-kitchen tips

- For beautifully browned pastry, bake the triangles on the top shelf of the oven.

- If you don't keep vegetable oil spray on hand, just brush or rub the lined baking sheet with oil.

On a flat work surface, unfold filo and cut lengthwise into 6 equal strips 2 to 3 inches wide. To prevent drying, cover filo strips with plastic wrap and top with a damp towel.

Brush 1 filo strip with melted butter. Place $\frac{1}{2}$ heaping teaspoon of the chicken mixture in 1 corner on a narrow end of the strip.

Fold the adjacent corner to the opposite edge, covering the filling and making a triangle. Continue folding the strip as you would fold a flag, keeping the triangular shape with each fold. Brush with butter and cover with plastic wrap to prevent drying. Repeat with remaining filo and filling. (If making in advance, refrigerate up to 8 hours. Freeze for longer storage.)

Preheat oven to 350°. Line a large baking sheet with foil or parchment paper; coat with vegetable oil spray. Place triangles about 1 inch apart on baking sheet. Bake until puffed and golden, 10 to 15 minutes. Let cool 5 minutes before serving.

stuffed easter eggs
uova ripiene pasquali from ITALIAN HOLIDAY COOKING

serves 8 | Antipasti are a specialty in the Piemonte region in northern Italy. Banquets sometimes begin with as many as thirty different kinds. While traveling there at Easter time, we were served several egg dishes as antipasti, including these delicious stuffed eggs.

8   large eggs

One 7-ounce can tuna in olive oil, drained

2   green onions, trimmed and cut into 1-inch pieces

2   tablespoons freshly grated Parmigiano-Reggiano

1   tablespoon drained capers

2 or 3 celery leaves

2 or 3 basil leaves

Salt and freshly ground black pepper

2   tablespoons extra virgin olive oil, or to taste

Chopped flat-leaf parsley for garnish

1   Place the eggs in a medium saucepan with water to cover and bring to a boil. Immediately turn off the heat. Leave the eggs in the pan until the water is cool enough to touch.

2   Drain the eggs and remove the shells. Cut them lengthwise in half, scoop out the yolks, and put them in a food processor or blender. Place the egg whites cut sides up on a serving plate.

3   Add the tuna, green onions, cheese, capers, celery, and basil to the egg yolks and chop fine. Add salt and pepper to taste. Drizzle in the olive oil and process until smooth. Taste for seasoning.

4   Spoon the egg yolk mixture into the egg whites. Sprinkle with parsley. Cover and chill until serving time.

wine match   Arneis, Vietti

FOOD & WINE test-kitchen tips

- If your capers are big, chop them a bit.

- So that you don't eat up too much of the filling by tasting to get the seasoning just right, it might be helpful to know that we found the mixture needed a teaspoon of salt. We also sprinkled a small pinch of salt in each egg-white hollow before stuffing it.

spanish potato omelet

tortillas de patata from ONE POTATO TWO POTATO

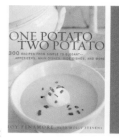

makes one 9-inch omelet | Not to be confused with Mexican tortillas, this is one of the truly great tapas of Spain and cousin to the Italian frittata. It's an omelet, and such a good one. You can cut it into squares or wedges, serve it warm or at room temperature or even cold, put it out with drinks, or have it for lunch. Leftover, it makes a great sandwich.

While I've given two variations of this recipe (see page 25), that's not the end of the story. Play with other combinations of flavors.

Yes, you can make this in a well-seasoned heavy skillet with sloping sides, but your life will be a lot easier if you use nonstick.

> 5   large eggs
>
> Coarse salt
>
> Potatoes for *Tortillas de Patata* (page 25), prepared either by stovetop
>   or by oven method and still hot
>
> 3   tablespoons olive oil (reserved oil, if you used the stovetop technique
>   for the potatoes)

Crack the eggs into a large bowl, add a pinch of salt, and beat them lightly with a fork. Add the hot cooked potatoes, pushing down to make sure they're completely covered by the eggs, and let sit for 15 to 20 minutes.

Spoon 2 tablespoons of the oil into a 9-inch nonstick skillet and turn the heat to medium-high. When the oil begins to smoke, add the eggs and potatoes. Press down with the back of a flexible spatula so no bits of potato stick out, and cook, shaking the pan frequently, until the bottom browns, about 5 minutes. Push the edges of the tortilla in with the back of your spatula, then slide the tortilla out onto a plate.

▼

FOOD & WINE test-kitchen tips

- If you use the stovetop method for cooking the potatoes, which we must say makes an especially delicious filling, the potatoes will absorb a lot of oil. Some of the oil comes out as the omelet cooks, so we recommend wearing protective oven mitts when you flip it.

wine recommendation A white wine with absolutely no oak is usually the best choice for egg dishes. Try an unoaked Chablis with this omelet or, for a festive occasion, Champagne.

Spoon the remaining 1 tablespoon oil into the skillet and heat until it starts to smoke. Cover the tortilla with another plate, flip it over, and slide it back into the skillet. Press down with the spatula again and tidy up the edges, pushing in with the back of the spatula. Keep shaking the pan, and cook until the second side is browned, about 4 minutes this time. Again slide it out onto a dish, invert it, and slip it back into the pan—you don't need more oil. Press down and neaten the edges. Cook for a minute, then flip it one last time.

Slide the tortilla out onto a clean plate and let it cool for at least 10 minutes before you cut it.

variations

spanish potato omelet with ham and mint Add 3 ounces finely chopped prosciutto or Black Forest ham, 1 garlic clove, minced, and 2½ teaspoons chopped fresh mint to the eggs when you beat them.

spanish potato omelet with parsley and garlic Add 2 garlic cloves, minced, and 3 tablespoons chopped flat-leaf parsley to the eggs when you beat them.

potatoes for tortillas de patata | According to Spanish cooking authority Penelope Casas, the classic technique for preparing potatoes to be used in a tortilla is the stovetop simmering-in-oil method. It does make a tasty, almost unctuous potato, but boy, does it use a lot of oil. So I'm also offering an oven method, one that I think results in an equally tasty potato. I've adapted both techniques from Casas.

¾ cup olive oil if using stovetop method, about 3 tablespoons
if using oven method

1–1¼ pounds russet potatoes, peeled and sliced ⅛ inch thick

Coarse salt

1 small onion, very thinly sliced

▼

stovetop method Pour the oil into a 9-inch skillet and heat it over medium heat until it shimmers. Carefully slip in a layer of potatoes, sprinkle with salt, and scatter with some of the onion. Repeat the layering until you've added all the potatoes and onion, then reduce the heat to medium-low. Cook gently, flipping the potatoes with a spatula from time to time, until very tender and just starting to break apart. This will take 20 to 35 minutes, depending on the age of the potatoes and just how you interpret "medium-low."

Drain the potatoes in a colander set over a bowl. Reserve the oil to use making the tortilla. Pat the potatoes dry with paper towels and proceed immediately with the tortilla recipe (see page 23).

oven method Heat the oven to 350 degrees. Use some of the oil to grease a 1½-quart gratin dish. Put in a layer of potatoes, sprinkle with salt, and scatter with some of the onion. Drizzle with oil. Repeat the layering until you've used all the potatoes and onions. Bake for 30 minutes, turn the potatoes with a spatula, and bake for another 15 minutes, or until the potatoes are tender (some will have started to brown at the edges). Proceed immediately with the tortilla recipe (see page 23), or one of the variations.

slow-roasted beet salad with parsley, celery, and fennel

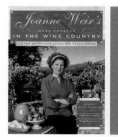

from JOANNE WEIR'S MORE COOKING IN THE WINE COUNTRY

serves 6 | Many people don't like beets, but I think that has to do with the way they are usually cooked. In fact, I'll never forget a woman in one of my cooking classes whose husband loved beets, but who hated them herself until she tried this recipe. (She maintained it saved her marriage.) Roasting accentuates the natural sweetness of beets. Here I put them together with parsley, celery, and fennel for a nice fall or winter salad.

1½ pounds red or gold beets, washed

1 tablespoon water

4 tablespoons extra virgin olive oil

1 cup flat-leaf parsley leaves

3 stalks celery, cut into very thin slices on the sharp diagonal

2 bulbs fennel, cut into paper-thin slices, feathery green tops chopped and reserved

½ small red onion, cut into thin rings

2 tablespoons white wine vinegar or Champagne vinegar

Salt and freshly ground black pepper

Preheat the oven to 350°F.

Place the beets in a shallow baking dish, and drizzle them with the water and 1 tablespoon of the olive oil. Roll the beets to coat them. Cover the pan with foil and roast until the beets are tender when pierced with a knife, 60 to 80 minutes. Let cool.

When the beets are cool enough to handle, peel and cut them into thin slices. Reserve.

▼

FOOD & WINE test-kitchen tips

- The easiest way to slice round vegetables, such as the beets and onions in this salad, is to cut them in half from top to bottom before you start slicing. That gives you a stable, flat surface to put on the cutting board. Rolling vegetables and sharp knives make a poor combination.

- We seasoned the vinaigrette with 1 teaspoon salt and ¼ teaspoon pepper. This may sound like a lot, but it's the only salt and pepper in the whole salad.

In a large bowl, toss together the parsley, celery, sliced fennel, and onion.

In another bowl, whisk together the vinegar and the remaining 3 tablespoons olive oil. Season with salt and pepper to taste. Toss three-fourths of the vinaigrette with the celery mixture, and let sit for 5 minutes. In the meantime, toss the remaining vinaigrette with the beets.

Place the celery mixture on a platter, top with the beets, and garnish with the reserved chopped fennel greens. Serve immediately.

wine suggestion Sauvignon Blanc

french beans with tarragon cream dressing and hazelnuts from A NEW WAY TO COOK

serves 4 | I've always loved the classic French salad of green beans in a lemony, heavy cream dressing. I replaced some of the heavy cream with sour cream and milk but still preserved the inimitable taste of cream. Since the dressing is quite thick and rich, you need only a small amount to coat the beans. Roasting intensifies the flavor of hazelnuts dramatically, so only a few per serving are needed to provide flavor—and crunch. This salad contains about half the calories of the classic version.

This dressing is also delicious on mild lettuces such as Buttercrunch and Boston.

$1/2$ ounce (12 to 15) hazelnuts

tarragon cream dressing
1   tablespoon plus 1 teaspoon heavy cream
1   tablespoon plus 1 teaspoon regular or reduced-fat sour cream
1   tablespoon plus 1 teaspoon whole milk
$1^1/2$ teaspoons fresh lemon juice
$1^1/2$ teaspoons minced fresh tarragon
1   teaspoon minced fresh chives
$1/4$ teaspoon kosher salt

$1/2$ teaspoon kosher salt
$1/2$ teaspoon sugar
1   pound haricots verts or young green beans, stem ends snapped off
Freshly ground black pepper
Fresh tarragon or chive sprigs for garnish (optional)

Preheat the oven to 400°F.

Spread the nuts on a small baking sheet or pie pan and roast, stirring them occasionally, until very fragrant and golden brown, 7 to 10 minutes. If it's possible, mist once or twice with a water spritzer to loosen the skins. Allow to cool slightly.

To remove the skins from the hazelnuts, pile them in a tea towel and rub them between your hands to remove the skins. Coarsely chop the hazelnuts and set aside.

To make the dressing, in a medium bowl, whisk together the heavy cream, sour cream, milk, lemon juice, tarragon, chives, and the ¼ teaspoon salt. Refrigerate for 1 hour before serving to let the flavors marry.

Bring a large pot of water to a boil over high heat. Stir in the ½ teaspoon salt and the sugar, add the beans, and boil until crisp-tender, about 5 minutes. Drain the beans and place them in a bowl of cold water. Run cold tap water over the beans until they are thoroughly cool. Drain well. Pat dry with paper towels.

Place the beans in a bowl and toss them with the dressing until completely coated. Add pepper to taste. Divide among four salad plates or shallow bowls and sprinkle with the hazelnuts. Garnish, if desired, with tarragon sprigs.

in advance You can make the dressing and prepare the beans up to 6 hours ahead; cover and refrigerate.

FOOD & WINE test-kitchen tips

- Don't be concerned if rubbing the toasted hazelnuts fails to remove every speck of the skin. It won't hurt you.

wine recommendation Whenever you're looking for a wine to pair with green vegetables, think of Grüner Veltliner from Austria. It has just the slightest hint of green-vegetable aroma. It also has enough acidity to cleanse your palate after a bite of even the creamiest sauce.

celery root and celery heart salad with blue cheese and glazed walnuts

from BAYWOLF RESTAURANT COOKBOOK

serves 4 | This salad is best prepared with young celery and small celery roots. Large celery roots tend to hollow out in the center and be tough on the outside. Celery, in each manifestation, is a clean, fresh vehicle for the richness of the cheese and the sweet crunch of the walnuts.

vinaigrette

1   shallot, minced

3   tablespoons sherry vinegar

Leaves from 1 thyme sprig, finely chopped

Salt and freshly ground black pepper

$^1/_2$ cup plus 1 tablespoon walnut oil

salad

2   pounds celery root, peeled and cut into thin triangles

4   small heads celery

1   tablespoon olive oil

1   cup walnuts

$1^1/_2$ tablespoons sugar

4   small handfuls Italian parsley leaves

Salt and freshly ground black pepper

7   ounces blue cheese, crumbled

to prepare the vinaigrette   Soak the shallot in the vinegar with the thyme, salt, and pepper for 25 minutes. Whisk in the walnut oil.

FOOD & WINE test-kitchen tips

- If you can't find all the ingredients called for here, this delicious first-course salad will still be excellent if you use: the white part of 4 scallions in place of the shallot, regular wine vinegar instead of sherry vinegar, and even peanut or another neutral oil in place of the walnut oil. You can also omit the fresh thyme.

- To cut celery root into thin triangles as suggested in this recipe, first cut it in $^1/_8$- to $^1/_4$-inch slices, then stack the slices and cut them into quarters.

wine recommendation   A crisp, aromatic white wine will serve these ingredients best. Think Riesling from Australia or California.

to prepare the salad Blanch the celery root until tender, then refresh in ice water. Drain and pat it dry with a towel. Trim the celery hearts 1 inch from the base. If the hearts are large, quarter and then blanch them as you did with the root. Marinate the roots and hearts in some of the vinaigrette. Take 4 of the celery stalks you just trimmed, and slice them thinly on an angle. Be sure to remove any fibrous strings. Heat the olive oil in a sauté pan, add the walnuts and sugar, and cook over medium heat until the sugar begins to caramelize. Do not let the nuts burn. Transfer to a plate to harden and cool.

to serve Add the walnuts, sliced celery, and parsley to the marinating roots and hearts. Season with salt and pepper, add a little more vinaigrette, and toss well. Garnish individual servings with the cheese.

hors d'oeuvres & first courses

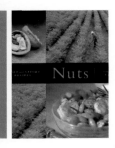

baby lima bean salad with shrimp and almonds **from NUTS**

serves 4 to 6 | Baby lima beans are more tender and less starchy than their more mature siblings, and their delicate flavor makes a fine match with the subtle sweetness of shrimp and almonds. You can even peel off the outer skin to reveal the bright green beans. Serve this salad as a first course, or as part of a composed salad or an antipasto platter. Or set it out at a picnic along with a nice bottle of chilled Sauvignon Blanc.

$^1/_2$ cup chopped almonds

7   tablespoons extra-virgin olive oil

1   package (20 ounces) frozen baby lima beans, thawed

1   tablespoon minced fresh rosemary

1   teaspoon minced fresh thyme

About $^3/_4$ teaspoon salt

2   large cloves garlic, minced

1   cup water

1   pound medium shrimp, shelled and deveined

2   large tomatoes (about 1 pound total), seeded and cut into $^1/_2$ inch cubes

3   tablespoons fresh lemon juice

About $^1/_2$ teaspoon freshly ground pepper

Lettuce leaves (optional)

Lemon wedges for garnish

Rosemary sprigs for garnish

Preheat oven to 350°. Spread almonds on a baking sheet or in a shallow pan. Bake, stirring once or twice, until lightly browned and fragrant, 8 to 10 minutes. Let cool.

▼

FOOD & WINE test-kitchen tips

- Though baby limas are very good indeed, we couldn't get them when we tested the recipe. This inspired salad is delectable even with standard frozen lima beans.

- When you toss the salad and taste for seasoning, you may find the dish needs salt. Add it courageously. We used a little more than a teaspoon at that point.

In a large frying pan, heat 1 tablespoon of the oil over medium heat. Add lima beans, rosemary, thyme, 1/2 teaspoon of the salt, and half of the garlic. Cook, stirring, until garlic is fragrant, 1 to 2 minutes. Pour in water; increase heat to medium-high and bring to a boil. Cook uncovered, stirring occasionally, until beans are just tender and liquid has evaporated, 3 to 5 minutes. Spoon bean mixture into a large bowl. Stir in 4 tablespoons more oil and let cool.

In the same pan, warm the remaining 2 tablespoons oil over medium heat. Add the remaining garlic and cook, stirring, until fragrant, about 1 minute. Add shrimp and 1/4 teaspoon salt. Increase heat to medium-high and cook, stirring, until shrimp are pink and opaque throughout, 3 to 4 minutes. Stir in tomatoes and cook, stirring, until just heated through, about 1 minute. Remove from heat and stir in the lemon juice. Let cool.

Add shrimp and cooking juices to the lima bean mixture, tossing gently to mix. Taste for seasoning, adding salt and pepper as needed.

Just before serving, stir in almonds. With a slotted spoon, spoon salad onto lettuce leaves or directly onto a platter. Garnish with lemon wedges and rosemary. Serve at cool room temperature.

roasted mushrooms
funghi ripieni from BIBA'S TASTE OF ITALY

serves 6 | My niece Daniela, who lives in Bologna with her husband, loves to cook and is always experimenting with what she calls *piatti facili*, easy dishes. When my husband and I had dinner at Daniela's house, the food she prepared was typical of what a young, busy working woman would cook midweek. Simple but delicious. These stuffed mushrooms were accompanied by a lovely glass of chilled prosecco.

1	pound large white mushrooms, wiped clean
1/3	cup extra virgin olive oil, plus extra for drizzling
1	garlic clove, finely minced
2	tablespoons chopped flat-leaf parsley
3 to 4 ounces thinly sliced mortadella or boiled ham, very finely minced
1/4	cup freshly grated Parmigiano-Reggiano
3	tablespoons fine dried bread crumbs
1	extra-large egg, lightly beaten
Salt and freshly ground black pepper to taste

Preheat the oven to 400°F.

Trim the mushrooms and separate the stems from the caps. Chop the stems very fine and set the caps aside.

Place the chopped stems in a small skillet with 2 tablespoons of the olive oil and cook, stirring, for a minute or two. Add the garlic and parsley, stir once or twice, and transfer to a small bowl. Add the mortadella, Parmigiano, bread crumbs, and egg. Season with salt and pepper and mix well. Stuff the mushroom caps with this mixture, mounding it slightly.

Smear the bottom of a baking dish large enough to hold the mushroom caps in a single layer with the remaining oil. Place the mushrooms in the dish and drizzle a bit of oil over each one.

Place the dish on the middle rack of the oven and bake for 15 to 20 minutes, or until the tops of the mushrooms are golden.

FOOD & WINE test-kitchen tips

- If you prefer not to taste for seasoning when a mixture contains raw egg, it may be useful to know that we used 1/2 teaspoon salt in the mushroom filling.

- The mushrooms can be stuffed a few hours ahead and refrigerated. Remove them from the refrigerator an hour before baking so they return to room temperature. Or simply increase the baking time.

cream of fennel soup

from HOME COOKING AROUND THE WORLD

makes 6 servings | As I mentioned in the Introduction to this book, I discovered the flavor of fish grilled over fennel branches long ago on the island of Corfu. After that, it was just a short leap to learning how to incorporate fennel seeds and fresh fennel into my own cooking.

This recipe is based on a soup I was served at La Pyramide, Fernand Point's legendary three-star restaurant in Vienne, France. There was nothing fancy about that version, and it was as simple as any *bonne femme* home-cooked rendition. By the time I had a chance to go to La Pyramide, Monsieur had died, and Madame was then in charge, still maintaining the high standards her husband had championed.

My version has few ingredients and only one spice in addition to the basic salt and pepper. The predominant flavor is that of the fennel, with no intricate parade of tastes as you take a spoonful, as there is in some of my recipes from Southeast Asia. Everything in the recipe is there just to accent the fennel. The soup is quite soothing and subtle.

The fennel available in today's markets is sweet fennel; its origins have been traced to Italy and the south of France. But through the Arab trade routes, both the stalk and especially the seed gained popularity in the Middle East, and then eventually spread to China via India, in much the same way spices traveled from India and Indonesia to Europe.

When at the suggestion of a friend I tried this cold, I discovered that it also makes a delicious summer soup.

3   large fennel bulbs (about 3 pounds)

2   tablespoons olive oil

1   yellow onion, thinly sliced

1   can (14.5 ounces) chicken broth, plus cold water to equal 4 cups, plus more water as needed

1$\frac{1}{2}$ teaspoons salt

$\frac{1}{4}$ teaspoon white pepper

$\frac{3}{4}$ cup heavy cream

$\frac{1}{8}$ teaspoon ground nutmeg

Fresh dill (optional)

Trim the stalks from the fennel bulbs and save for future use, such as in salads or for braising. Reserve some of the feathery fronds for a garnish, if desired. Halve the bulbs through the root end, cut out the core, and thinly slice halves crosswise.

In a large saucepan, heat the olive oil. Add the onion and sauté until it just begins to brown, about 5 minutes. Add sliced fennel, plus about 2 tablespoons of the broth with water. Cover pan and "sweat" or cook the fennel over medium heat until it is slightly tender, 10 to 15 minutes, stirring from time to time. Add the salt and white pepper. Add the remaining chicken broth with water to cover the fennel, adding more water if needed. Bring to a boil. Lower heat, partially cover saucepan, and simmer until fennel is very tender, about 30 minutes.

Drain fennel in a colander set over a large bowl and reserve the cooking liquid. Working in batches, spoon solids into a food processor. Process, adding as much of the cooking liquid as needed to make a smooth puree. Wipe out saucepan with a paper towel and transfer puree to pan. Stir in enough of reserved cooking liquid for desired consistency. (My preference is to keep the soup slightly thick.) Stir in the heavy cream and nutmeg. Gently reheat, and serve garnished with fennel fronds and chopped fresh dill, if desired. Or refrigerate soup and serve chilled.

serving tip This soup is delicious either warm or chilled, depending on the weather and your taste. It makes a perfect light lunch or a first course, with a small salad of bitter greens, such as radicchio, Belgian endive, and/or kale.

FOOD & WINE test-kitchen tips

- If the finished soup is too thick for your taste, even after stirring in all the cooking liquid, just add some water—up to $1/3$ cup. More than that is likely to start watering down the flavor.

wine recommendation Although Orvieto's reputation has been tarnished by many poor bottles, a good-quality Orvieto is a wonderful accompaniment to many vegetable dishes and works particularly well with the sweet flavor of fennel.

root vegetable crema

serves 4 | This puree of root vegetables is adapted from one by Paul Bertolli when he was chef at Chez Panisse in Berkeley, California. The root vegetables are slowly braised in water with a little butter, so the small amount of fat gives them a rich texture.

Although this soup is delicious as is, an optional tablespoon of heavy cream or crème fraîche per serving gives it a luxurious finish (even with this splurge, a serving weighs in at under 150 calories).

2	teaspoons unsalted butter
1	medium yellow or red waxy potato, thinly sliced ($3/4$ cup)
1	small celery root, finely diced ($3/4$ cup)
1	medium leek, white part only, thinly sliced and rinsed ($1/4$ cup)
2	small parsnips, halved lengthwise, woody core removed, and finely sliced ($1/2$ cup)
2	garlic cloves, thinly sliced
1	sprig fresh thyme
$1/4$	teaspoon kosher salt
$1/4$	teaspoon sugar
$2/3$	cup water
3	cups unsalted homemade or canned low-sodium chicken broth
	Freshly ground white pepper
	A few gratings of nutmeg (optional)
$1/4$	cup heavy cream or crème fraîche, lightly whipped (optional)

Melt the butter in a medium saucepan over moderate heat. Add the potato, celery root, leek, parsnips, garlic, thyme, salt, sugar, and water and bring to a simmer. Cover and cook for 15 minutes, or until almost all the water has evaporated. Add the chicken broth, bring back to a simmer, cover, and cook for an additional 15 minutes, or until the vegetables are soft.

FOOD & WINE test-kitchen tips

- This vegetable soup is pretty thick, as is the fashion now. If you'd like a thinner puree, add a bit of water to the finished soup. We added about $1/2$ cup.

wine recommendation A crisp, dry Vouvray from the Loire region of France will be light enough so it won't overwhelm the delicate vegetable flavors of this dish yet have enough acidity to leave the palate refreshed.

For the finest texture, puree the soup, in batches, in a blender. If you are using a food processor, let it run for at least 2 minutes. Strain the soup back into the saucepan. Season to taste with white pepper, nutmeg, and additional salt, if necessary. Swirl some of the cream, if using, into each serving.

in advance   You can prepare the soup 3 days ahead; cover and refrigerate. Or freeze it for up to 2 months.

variation

root vegetable soup with truffles   Root vegetables have a special affinity for truffles. Pound all or part of a fresh black truffle to a paste in a mortar and add to the soup. A drizzle of white truffle oil is also divine.

tuscan minestrone with black kale and chickpeas

from BAYWOLF RESTAURANT COOKBOOK

serves 8 to 10 | Soup should be salted as you go along. Salting only at the end is like salting only the outside of the soup. Layering and salting gradually produces a multi-dimensional dish. That is what we're looking for. This soup is best if it is made at least one day in advance. It takes a while to cook and will be drastically compromised if you try to make it quickly.

3	tablespoons olive oil
$1/2$	cup diced pancetta
2	onions, diced
1	carrot, peeled and diced
2	celery stalks, diced
1	small fennel bulb, diced
1	bunch purple kale, chopped
1	bay leaf

An herb bundle containing thyme, savory, and oregano

2	salt-packed anchovies, filleted, rinsed, and chopped

2 to 3 tablespoons chopped garlic

1	tablespoon tomato paste
10	cups poultry stock, heated
1	cup cooked chickpeas
3	dried porcini mushrooms
$1/4$	teaspoon ground cinnamon

Sherry vinegar to taste

2	tablespoons chopped Italian parsley

Shaved Parmesan cheese

FOOD & WINE test-kitchen tips

- We couldn't get purple kale when we tested this recipe, so we made it with regular green. The soup was excellent.

- We also used canned chickpeas rather than cooking dry ones. If you do this, though, be sure to rinse them well.

wine recommendation   Vernaccia, a dry white wine from Tuscany, will be the perfect foil for this hearty soup.

Heat the oil with the pancetta in a large, heavy-bottomed pot over medium-high heat. Cook gently until the pancetta is light brown but not crispy. Add the onions and cook over medium heat for about 15 minutes, or until lightly browned. During this cooking time, scrape the bottom of the pan for the caramelized bits. These bits are what will make your soup really good. Don't burn them. Add the carrot and cook for 10 minutes more, scraping occasionally, then cook the celery for 10 minutes, then the fennel for 10 minutes. The vegetables will shrink down quite a bit. Add the kale, bay leaf, and herbs, and cook until the kale has wilted. Add the anchovies and garlic and sweat some more. Add the tomato paste and half the stock. Bring to a boil, then reduce to a simmer.

Purée the chickpeas with the remaining stock, and then add to the soup. Boil the dried mushrooms with some of the soup in a separate pot until tender. Purée thoroughly and add back to the soup. Simmer for 20 minutes. Add the cinnamon, then simmer for another 20 minutes. Adjust the seasoning and finish with vinegar. Remove the herb bundle.

Just before serving, stir in the parsley. Garnish each bowl with shaved Parmesan.

ecuadorian potato-cheese soup with avocado

from HOME COOKING AROUND THE WORLD

makes 8 servings | Harrison, New Jersey, is a town on the Passaic River across from Newark. A walk down its main street takes you past an assortment of restaurants: Brazilian, Portuguese, Ecuadorian, Italian, and Polish. One of the Ecuadorian restaurants serves breakfast, lunch, and dinner, seven days a week, and on Sundays, it is full of young families surrounded by huge platters of food. It was there that I discovered this richly satisfying soup with its bright, sunny color. It's called *locro*, but it's different from the Argentine *locro*, and also contains most of the same ingredients as *Papas a la Huancaina* from Peru, Ecuador's neighbor to the south. When a Danish friend of mine tasted this soup, she remarked that it reminded her of a similar soup that she grew up with in Denmark, but hers had peas.

For a meatier version, I've made this soup with a pound of shredded cooked chicken stirred in.

2	tablespoons unsalted butter
1	medium-size yellow onion, chopped
1	teaspoon Hungarian sweet paprika
¼	teaspoon turmeric
4	cups cold water
2	teaspoons salt
¼	teaspoon black pepper
4	large Yukon Gold potatoes (about 2 pounds) *or* other boiling potatoes, peeled and cut into ½-inch-thick slices
2	cups light cream
2	cups corn kernels, fresh *or* frozen, thawed
1	cup crumbled *queso blanco* (firmly packed fresh cheese) *or* crumbled farmer's cheese *or* grated Muenster cheese (about ¼ pound)
2	medium-size ripe avocados
	Snipped fresh chives *or* fresh cilantro leaves, for garnish

In a large saucepan, heat the butter over medium heat. Add the onion, paprika, and turmeric and sauté until onion is softened, about 4 to 5 minutes. Add the water, salt, and pepper. Bring to a boil. Add the potatoes. Lower heat and simmer, covered, until potatoes are tender, about 25 minutes.

▼

Break up potatoes into smaller pieces with a fork or wooden spoon. Stir in the cream and corn and cook until heated through and corn is tender, about 4 minutes. Stir in the cheese and heat until melted, about 1 minute.

Halve, peel, and pit the avocados. Slice crosswise. Place avocado pieces in soup bowls. Ladle soup over the avocado slices, garnish with snipped fresh chives or cilantro leaves, and serve.

FOOD & WINE test-kitchen tips

- To pit an avocado easily, cut it in half, stick the knife into the pit, and twist.

- This luscious soup reheats surprisingly well, so you can make it ahead of time. Just wait to add the avocado and herbs until you serve.

- Though we put this soup in the first-course chapter—and it makes a fine first course—we can also happily make a meal of it.

wine recommendation One of the best accompaniments to almost any soup is Brut Champagne, which is also a particular friend to avocado.

steamed mussels in roasted tomato–saffron broth **from BOBBY FLAY COOKS AMERICAN**

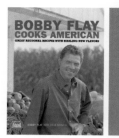

serves 4 | To bring out all the tastes in this simple dish, I first make a flavorful broth to steam the mussels in. With its roasted tomatoes and aromatic saffron, the savory broth becomes as much a part of the dish as the juicy mussels. Don't forget to put out some crusty bread—everybody loves to dunk when they get to the bottom of the bowl. It makes for a fun, family-style dish.

for the roasted tomatoes

8   plum tomatoes, halved and seeded

6   cloves garlic, peeled

3   tablespoons olive oil

Salt and freshly ground pepper

for the soup

2   tablespoons olive oil

1   onion, thinly sliced

1   cup dry white wine

3   cups Shrimp Stock (page 49) or bottled clam juice

Pinch of saffron

Salt and freshly ground pepper

48   cultivated mussels, scrubbed and debearded

¼   cup chopped flat leaf parsley

1 Make the roasted tomatoes: Preheat the oven to 350°F. Toss the tomatoes and garlic with the 3 tablespoons olive oil in a shallow baking pan. Season with salt and pepper to taste. Roast until very soft, 25–30 minutes or more. Transfer the tomatoes, garlic, and any accumulated juices to a food processor and puree until smooth.

▼

FOOD & WINE test-kitchen tips

- The portions here are for a first course. The recipe will serve two as a main dish.

wine recommendation   Mussels and Muscadet are a classic combination. The high acidity of the Muscadet grape will do a superb job of standing up to the tomato-based broth here.

2 Make the soup: Heat the 2 tablespoons olive oil in a large saucepan over high heat. Add the onion and cook, stirring often, until soft. Add the wine and cook until reduced by three-fourths. Add the shrimp stock or clam juice and saffron and bring to a boil. Add the roasted tomato puree, season with salt and pepper, and bring to a boil.

3 Add the mussels, cover the pot, and cook until all the mussels have opened, 3–5 minutes. Discard any mussels that have not opened. Divide the mussels among 4 bowls and keep warm. Raise the heat under the broth to high and cook until reduced by half. Stir in the parsley and ladle the broth over the mussels. Serve immediately.

shrimp stock | makes 4–5 cups

2	tablespoons olive oil
3	cups raw shrimp shells and tails
1	large onion, coarsely chopped
1	small carrot, coarsely chopped
$1/2$	celery stalk, coarsely chopped
1	cup white wine
1	tomato, coarsely chopped, or $1/4$ cup canned plum tomatoes
1	bay leaf
6	cups cold water

In a large pot, heat the oil over high heat until almost smoking. Add the shrimp shells, onion, carrot, and celery, and cook, stirring, 5 minutes. Add the remaining ingredients and the cold water and bring to a boil. Reduce the heat to a simmer and cook, partly covered, 40 minutes. Strain through cheesecloth or a fine strainer, let cool, and refrigerate up to 2 days or freeze.

fettuccine with sweet corn and gorgonzola

from SECOND HELPINGS FROM UNION SQUARE CAFE

serves 6 as an appetizer, 4 as a main course | This has long been a late-summer pasta staple at Union Square Cafe. We encourage you to make your own fresh fettuccine as we do at the restaurant, but for ease, you'll be more than satisfied using a good-quality dried egg fettuccine. For the sauce, we've borrowed a *truc* from classic corn chowder recipes, steeping corncobs with white wine and cream, to lend a richly complex, sweet corn flavor. The addition of roasted tomatoes, Gorgonzola, and pancetta completes one of our very favorite pasta sauces.

2	large ears sweet corn
1	tablespoon olive oil
2	ounces pancetta, diced (about $^1/_2$ cup)
$^1/_2$	cup sliced shallots
1	tablespoon coarsely chopped garlic
$^1/_2$	cup white wine
2	cups heavy cream
	Kosher salt
2	tablespoons Gorgonzola cheese
$^1/_8$	teaspoon freshly ground black pepper
12	Oven-Dried Tomatoes, cut in half lengthwise (next page)
$^1/_2$	cup sliced (on the diagonal) scallions, white and green parts
$^1/_3$	cup sliced basil leaves
1	pound egg fettuccine

1 Cut the kernels off the corncobs by standing each corncob on its flat end on a cutting board or in a roasting pan, and slicing down against the cob. Set the kernels aside. Cut the cobs into 2-inch sections.

FOOD & WINE test-kitchen tips

- The Gorgonzola called for here honors the Italian inspiration of the dish, but any creamy blue cheese will be fine.

- If you don't have time to make the oven-dried tomatoes called for in this recipe, you can just buy good-quality sun-dried ones. If you make that substitution, you might want to cut back on the salt in the dish.

2 Combine the oil and pancetta in a 2-quart saucepan and cook over medium-high heat to render the fat and crisp the pancetta, about 5 minutes. Remove the pancetta with a slotted spoon and set aside. Discard all but 1 tablespoon of the fat.

3 Reduce the heat to medium. Add the shallots, garlic, and corncobs and cook until the shallots are softened but not browned, about 3 minutes. Pour in the wine and reduce until almost dry. Add the cream and simmer very gently for 5 minutes. Remove from the heat, cover, and let the sauce steep for at least 15 minutes.

4 Bring 4 quarts of water to a boil in a large pot and add 2 tablespoons salt.

5 Strain the sauce through a fine-mesh strainer into a straight-sided skillet or saucepan large enough to hold all the pasta. Place over medium heat and whisk in the cheese in small pieces. Season with 1 teaspoon of salt and the pepper. Add the pancetta, corn kernels, tomatoes, scallions, and basil. Bring to a simmer, turn off the heat, cover, and set aside.

6 Cook the fettuccine in the boiling water until *al dente*, and drain in a colander. Add the drained pasta to the sauce and toss until the pasta is well coated. Transfer to a platter and serve hot.

wine suggestions This works well with fruity whites like tocai friulano or chardonnay, or with a youthful red like Barbera d'Alba or Valpolicella Classico.

oven-dried tomatoes | **makes 1 1/2 cups** | Plum tomatoes have won acceptance primarily as an ingredient for making cooked tomato sauce. Their sturdiness also makes them superb candidates for enduring a long, slow day in the oven. These roasted plum tomatoes can be enjoyed any way you've ever used sun-dried tomatoes, but they're even more versatile, since they're a lot less salty.

▼

51

2	pounds ripe plum tomatoes, washed, cored, and split lengthwise
1	teaspoon kosher salt
2	cups extra-virgin olive oil
2	large fresh thyme sprigs
1	fresh rosemary branch, split
2 to 3 sage leaves	
3	medium garlic cloves, peeled and split

1 Place the tomatoes, cut side up, on a baking sheet. Sprinkle with the salt and let sit for 1 hour.

2 Preheat the oven to 200 degrees F.

3 Roast the tomatoes for 5 to 6 hours. The tomatoes are done when they are dried, but still slightly plump; they should definitely not be leathery, nor as dry as commercial sun-dried tomatoes.

4 Allow the tomatoes to cool to room temperature; then transfer them to a jar or bowl. Stir in the olive oil, herbs, and garlic. Cover tightly, and refrigerate. The tomatoes will improve if marinated for 2 to 3 days before using. They will keep for up to 2 weeks in the refrigerator.

sheep's-milk ricotta gnocchi from SECOND HELPINGS FROM UNION

SQUARE CAFE | serves 6 to 8 | This recipe is a delicious variation on the traditional potato gnocchi. The sheep's-milk ricotta and mascarpone, lightly bound with egg and a touch of flour, create cloudlike puffs, beautifully complemented by a green and white sauce with a gently acidic edge of lemon and verjus—the juice of unripened grapes. Even if you are using them immediately, you might want to consider lightly freezing the gnocchi, as this makes them easier to handle while cooking.

gnocchi

15 ounces sheep's-milk ricotta, or cow's-milk ricotta, drained in a colander for at least 1 hour

$^1/_4$ cup mascarpone

2 large eggs

$^1/_2$ cup grated Pecorino Romano

$^1/_2$ cup grated Parmigiano-Reggiano

Kosher salt

Pinch of freshly ground pepper

Pinch of freshly grated nutmeg

$^1/_2$ cup plus 2 tablespoons all-purpose flour, plus extra for dusting

lemon-spinach sauce

1 lemon

$1^1/_2$ tablespoons butter

1 medium onion, thinly sliced

1 celery stalk, sliced

$^1/_2$ cup verjus or dry white wine

2 cups heavy cream

$^1/_2$ teaspoon kosher salt

$^1/_8$ teaspoon freshly ground pepper

Pinch of freshly grated nutmeg

1 packed cup stemmed spinach leaves, cut into $^1/_2$-inch strips

$^1/_4$ cup plus 2 tablespoons grated Pecorino Romano

1 Make the gnocchi: Combine the ricotta and mascarpone in a food processor and process until smooth. Add the eggs, the two grated cheeses, the salt, pepper, and nutmeg, and blend until smooth. Transfer the mixture to a large bowl. Gently fold in the flour in 2 batches with a rubber spatula just until the flour is incorporated and the dough has the consistency of a stiff mousse. To avoid tough gnocchi, don't overwork the dough.

2 Sprinkle a cookie sheet with flour.

3 Spoon the dough into a pastry bag fitted with a ¾-inch plain tip (#808). Squeeze out a 1-inch cylinder of dough and cut it onto the cookie sheet, forming evenly spaced rows of gnocchi. This is easily done by dipping a paring knife in warm water, then slicing down cleanly through the dough with the blade pressing against the pastry tip. Once you've cut all the gnocchi, refrigerate until ready to cook. (The gnocchi can also be frozen at this point. To do this, first freeze them on the cookie sheet, then store in zip-top bags. Do not defrost before cooking.)

4 Make the sauce: Grate the zest from the lemon and squeeze 2 tablespoons of juice. Reserve the zest and juice separately.

5 Melt the butter in a 2-quart saucepan (large enough to eventually hold the gnocchi) over medium heat. Add the onion and celery and cook until wilted, but not browned, about 4 minutes. Add the verjus or white wine and the reserved lemon juice. Bring to a boil and reduce until almost dry, about 10 minutes. Add the cream and boil, reducing until it coats the back of a spoon, about 10 to 12 minutes. Strain the sauce into a bowl, and season with the salt, pepper, and nutmeg. Stir in the reserved lemon zest and set aside.

FOOD & WINE test-kitchen tips

- Don't hesitate to make the substitutions suggested in this recipe. We used white wine rather than verjus and plain-old supermarket-variety ricotta cheese. The gnocchi were superbly tender and delicious.

- You'll need to add about 1 teaspoon of salt to the gnocchi dough.

- A wide metal spatula is the best implement for transferring several raw gnocchi at once to the boiling water.

- Gnocchi lovers that we are, we could make dinner of this dish alone. It will serve six as an informal main course.

6 Bring 4 quarts of water to a boil and add 2 tablespoons of salt. Gently transfer the gnocchi to the water and boil until they are completely cooked through and firm to the touch, 5 minutes. Remove with a slotted spoon and drain in a colander.

7 Return the sauce to the saucepan and bring to a simmer over medium heat. Add the spinach and cook until wilted, about 2 minutes. Add the gnocchi and heat through, tossing gently to coat with the sauce. Spoon into warm bowls and top with the cheese. Serve immediately.

wine suggestions A youthful sauvignon blanc like Sancerre or Pouilly Fumé would be an ideal partner for the gnocchi, as would a pinot bianco or Müller-Thurgau from Friuli–Venezia Giulia.

hors d'oeuvres & first courses

polenta with soft cheese and browned butter *toc'n braide*

from ITALIAN HOLIDAY COOKING

serves 4 | This version of polenta, topped with soft cheese and browned butter, is from the Friuli–Venezia Giulia region of northeastern Italy. Made with milk, it is softer and creamier than other polentas. Though it is very simple, it is also very rich and should stand alone as a first course, not a side dish.

1   cup fine yellow cornmeal, preferably stone-ground

1   cup milk

Salt

topping

3/4   cup ricotta

2   tablespoons soft fresh goat cheese

3   tablespoons unsalted butter

1   tablespoon fine yellow cornmeal

Pinch of salt

1 In a bowl, stir together the cornmeal and 2 cups cold water.

2 In a large heavy saucepan, bring the milk to a simmer. Add the cornmeal. Cook, stirring until the mixture comes to a gentle simmer. Lower the heat (place the pan over a Flame Tamer if necessary to keep the polenta from scorching). Cook, stirring occasionally, for 30 to 40 minutes, until the polenta has thickened and lost its raw taste. It should be pourable; if it is too thick, add a little water. Add salt to taste.

3 While the polenta is cooking, make the topping: whisk the cheeses in a bowl until smooth. Just before the polenta is done, melt the butter in a small skillet. Add the 1 tablespoon cornmeal and the salt and cook, swirling the pan, until the cornmeal is toasted and lightly browned.

FOOD & WINE test-kitchen tips

- To keep the spirit of this dish, use regular milk and ricotta, not low-fat.

- Depending on the brand and age of the cornmeal you use, you may need more or less water. We had to add a cup—and even more is fine. The important thing is that the mixture remains fluid.

4 Spoon the polenta into four soup plates. Top with the cheese mixture and drizzle with the melted butter. Serve immediately.

tip To clean the pot after cooking polenta, fill it with cold water and 2 tablespoons of powdered dishwasher soap. Let soak for 30 minutes to 1 hour. Any residue comes off right away.

wine match Pinot Bianco, Castello di Spessa

lemon risotto with peas, parsley, prosciutto, and parmesan

from BAYWOLF RESTAURANT COOKBOOK

serves 4 | Some of the BayWolf's most delicious dishes have been developed out of my communicable affection for the use of alliteration in the written menus. This felicitous combination sounds so edible and appealing even before you indulge in the first taste.

1   tablespoon olive oil

2   tablespoons butter

½   medium onion, diced

1   generous cup Arborio rice

1   cup dry white wine

4   cups chicken stock, heated

Salt and freshly ground black pepper

Finely chopped zest of 2 lemons

1   cup shelled peas, blanched

½   cup freshly grated Parmesan cheese

1   handful Italian parsley, roughly chopped

Freshly squeezed lemon juice

4   prosciutto slices, julienned

FOOD & WINE test-kitchen tips

- Most of the year, frozen peas are better than fresh. If you use frozen in this risotto, just rinse them under hot water to thaw them. There's no need to blanch the peas as you would fresh ones, because they're already cooked before they're frozen.

- If you want to serve this as a main course, the recipe will serve two.

wine recommendation   Italy has a number of native white wines that are well-kept secrets. They tend to be good food wines and are almost never a strain on the budget. Here, a Greco di Tufo or a Vermentino will work magic.

Heat the fats in a large saucepan until hot and bubbly, then add the onion. Cook over medium heat until translucent. Don't let the onion brown. Add the rice and fry for a minute, stirring constantly. Add the wine and reduce for a few minutes. Over medium-low heat, add 1 cup of the stock, and season lightly with salt, pepper, and lemon zest. Stir occasionally while the rice absorbs the stock. Add another cup of stock and proceed in the same fashion until all of the stock has been added and the rice is just done. This will take 25 to 30 minutes. Stir in the peas, Parmesan, and parsley. Adjust the seasoning with salt, pepper, and lemon juice. Keep in mind that the prosciutto will provide some of the salt. Right before serving, stir in the prosciutto. It should not cook. Serve immediately.

risotto with eggplant, anchovy, and mint

from SECOND HELPINGS FROM UNION SQUARE CAFE

serves 4 to 6 | Here's a risotto variation whose bold flavors remind us of the food of Rome's Jewish quarter. Anchovies, pecorino, and mint wake up the subtle, musky eggplant, which almost melts right into the creamy rice. As a starter, this risotto would be a natural before lamb or chicken, or enjoy it as a main course accompanied by a simple salad of bitter greens like arugula, dandelion, or radicchio.

Kosher salt

1 or 2 medium eggplants, unpeeled, cut into $^1/_2$-inch dice (4 cups)

$^1/_3$ cup plus 2 tablespoons extra-virgin olive oil

6 cups Chicken Stock (page 161)

2 tablespoons minced shallots

1 teaspoon garlic

5 anchovy fillets, minced

$1^3/_4$ cups arborio rice

1 cup white wine

3 tablespoons chopped fresh mint

3 tablespoons butter

$^1/_2$ cup grated Pecorino Romano

$^1/_8$ teaspoon freshly ground pepper

1 Combine 1 quart of cold water and 2 tablespoons of salt in a large bowl. Add the diced eggplant and let soak for 30 minutes. Drain well in a colander.

2 In a large sauté pan, heat $^1/_3$ cup of the oil over medium-high heat until very hot, and add the drained eggplant. If your sauté pan is not large enough to hold all the eggplant in one layer, do this step in more than one batch. Cook the eggplant until well browned and tender, 8 to 10 minutes. Stir often during the last half of cooking, and reduce the heat as needed to keep the eggplant from burning. Transfer to a dish and set aside.

FOOD & WINE test-kitchen tips

- If your rice is quite dry (as it often is in the winter or when it's been around for a while), it may take longer to cook. Ours needed about 35 minutes. When we ran out of stock, we just added water to keep the risotto moist.

- To test rice, break a grain. The moment the center turns from opaque (raw) to translucent, the risotto is done.

3 In a small saucepan, bring the chicken stock to a simmer.

4 Combine 2 tablespoons of oil, the shallots, garlic, and anchovies in a 3-quart, heavy-bottomed saucepan or skillet. Place over medium heat and stir to cook, without coloring, about 2 minutes. Add the rice and 1 teaspoon of salt, and stir with a wooden spoon until the rice is coated with the oil. Add the wine and bring to a boil over medium-high heat; cook the rice, stirring constantly, until it absorbs the wine.

5 Ladle ½ cup of the simmering broth into the saucepan and stir until it is absorbed. Continue with the rest of the broth, adding ½ cup at a time and letting each addition become absorbed completely into the rice before adding more liquid. The constant stirring allows the rice to release its starch into the cooking liquid, resulting in the characteristic risotto creaminess. Count on approximately 20 to 25 minutes for the rice to be cooked *al dente*.

6 Fold in the eggplant and cook until heated through, about 30 seconds. Add the mint, swirl in the butter and half the cheese, and season with ½ teaspoon of salt and the pepper. Spoon the risotto onto a warm platter or into individual bowls, sprinkle with the remaining pecorino, and serve immediately.

wine suggestions To soften the bitterness of eggplant, pick a red wine with ample tannins and fruit. Try a Montepulciano d'Abruzzo or Sardinian cannonau from Italy, or from France, a syrah or grenache-based wine from Provence or the Rhône Valley.

risotto pancake
risotto al salto from ENOTECA

serves 8 | Leftover risotto can be turned into pancakes that are cut into wedges and sauced. They can be stuffed with cheeses, sauteéd mushrooms, and sausage. Also called *tortino di riso*, unstuffed rice pancakes are served with a variety of sauces at the Vineria Cozzi in Bergamo Alto.

rice

1   cup Arborio rice

1$^1/_2$ cups water

1   teaspoon salt

2   eggs, lightly beaten

$^1/_3$ cup grated Parmesan cheese

Freshly ground black pepper

pancake

1$^1/_2$ cups diced Fontina cheese

$^1/_4$ cup chopped hazelnuts

1   tablespoon chopped fresh sage or marjoram

4 to 6 tablespoons unsalted butter or olive oil

To make the rice, in a saucepan combine the rice, water, and salt. Bring to a boil over high heat, cover, reduce the heat to low, and cook until the rice is tender and all the water is absorbed, 15 to 18 minutes. Stir in the eggs and Parmesan and season to taste with pepper. You probably won't need much salt, as the cheese is fairly salty. Spoon the rice mixture onto a baking sheet and refrigerate until cool.

To make the pancake, combine the cheese, nuts, and sage or marjoram in a bowl and mix well. Warm 3 tablespoons of the butter or oil in a 10-inch, nonstick sauté pan over medium heat. Add half of the rice, packing it down. Top with the cheese mixture, spreading it evenly. Then layer the remaining rice on top, pressing it down with a fork. Cook, shaking the pan from time to time, until the bottom of the pancake is golden brown, 5 to 7 minutes.

FOOD & WINE test-kitchen tips

- If hazelnuts are hard to find, almonds will do. They're more delicate in flavor but will add the requisite texture.

- We used the Tomato Sauce recipe on page 81 to top this crunchy risotto pancake.

Slide the pancake out onto a plate. Add more butter or oil to the pan as needed to prevent sticking, and return the pan to the heat. When hot, slip the pancake, browned side up, back into the pan and cook until the second side is golden, about 5 minutes longer.

Slide onto a serving platter. Let rest for a few minutes, then cut into wedges and serve warm. The wedges may also be reheated for 10 minutes in a 350°F oven.

matching pointer This tasty pancake is just a delivery for a sauce. If leaning toward a tomato-based sauce, look for a sharper red wine. If going with a cream base, select a zesty, flavorful white. **italian wines** Barbera d'Asti, Rosso di Montepulciano, Franciacorta, Soave **alternative wines** Barbera (California), Sauvignon Blanc (France, New Zealand)

piquant shrimp

gambas picantes philippines

from MADHUR JAFFREY'S STEP-BY-STEP COOKING

serves 4 as a main course, or 6 as a first course | This dish is Spanish in its origins, like so many other Filipino dishes. It is served in some of Manila's most distinguished restaurants as an appetizer. I often serve it as a main course with rice and a simple vegetable side dish. If you prefer a milder flavor, you can substitute ⅓ cup finely chopped bell green pepper for the chilies.

1 pound medium shrimp

1 teaspoon paprika

5 garlic cloves

1 to 2 fresh hot green chilies

4 tablespoons olive oil

½ teaspoon salt

Freshly ground black pepper

1 Peel and devein the shrimp. Rinse them, pat dry, and put them in a bowl. Add the paprika and toss to mix. Peel the garlic and chop it finely. Chop the chilies finely.

2 Put the oil in a wok or large frying pan and set it over high heat. When the oil is hot, add the garlic and stir-fry for 30 seconds or until it turns golden.

3 Add the shrimp and green chilies. Stir-fry over high heat for 2 to 3 minutes or until the shrimp turn opaque all the way through. Add the salt and pepper. Toss again and serve.

FOOD & WINE test-kitchen tips

- Five cloves of garlic sounds like a lot for a pound of shrimp. Trust the recipe. Our tasters were entirely surprised when we told them how much garlic was in the dish.

- We kept a few Piquant Shrimp to taste later. We liked them even better the next day at room temperature; they'd make an ideal hors d'oeuvre for a party.

wine recommendation Look for a Semillon–Sauvignon Blanc blend from Australia. The unctuous Semillon will help soothe the effect of the spicy red pepper, and the Sauvignon Blanc will provide enough acidity to leave the palate refreshed.

The Spanish ruled the Philippines from 1521 until 1898. At that point the Americans took over, staying through the Second World War until 1946. The Spanish occupation not only gave the Philippines its name (the country is named after Philip II of Spain) and its major religion, Catholicism, but introduced a Mediterranean style of eating. Spanish food was mostly cooked in olive oil, with seasonings limited to garlic, onions, tomatoes, bell peppers, and vinegar. The Filipinos began to add Spanish ingredients to their own recipes and to cook the newcomers' fancy food as well. They thought it rather grand, however, to call most dishes by Spanish names, especially on menus.

meat

herb-scented tuscan pork roast from **A NEW WAY TO COOK**

serves 8 | At Peggy Markel's cooking school, La Cucina al Focolore, eighteen miles southeast of Florence, a pork roast is boned and seasoned with sage-and-rosemary salt, then placed on a rack of the bones, which add flavor to the meat and pan juices. As it roasts, it is basted with white wine, both to build up a caramelized surface and to provide a pan sauce, a technique used for all manner of roasts in Tuscany. My American adaptation of this recipe is to cover the roast with thin slices of pancetta, which give it the juiciness and savor of Italian pork.

If you ask the butcher to saw through the chine bone that holds the ribs together, the ribs will roast into a rack of delectable spare ribs, which you can cut apart to nibble on. (Bear in mind that since ribs are quite rich, they will up the fat and calorie count.)

This is a wonderful dinner party dish, because it takes so little work for such a dramatic effect. It is also delicious cold.

One 7-pound pork loin, boned (have the butcher do this,
    reserving the bones; see above), fat trimmed
Tuscan Herb Salt (page 70)
Four 10-inch-long rosemary branches
1 1/2 teaspoons kosher salt
3 ounces (4 to 5 thin slices) lean pancetta
1 teaspoon olive oil
2 cups dry white wine
Kosher salt and freshly ground black pepper

Pat the pork loin dry. Using a knife-sharpening steel or a long-handled wooden spoon, pierce a hole lengthwise through the center of the loin. Working from either end of the loin, use your fingers to stuff all but 1 tablespoon of the herb salt into the hole. Insert 1 of the rosemary branches into each end so that it forms a tassle. Mix the remaining herb salt with the 1 1/2 teaspoons salt and rub it all over the roast.

FOOD & WINE test-kitchen tips

- We used a wooden spoon to pierce a hole through the middle of the roast, as directed, and also found the handle convenient to distribute the herb salt throughout the hole.

wine recommendation Staying with the Tuscan theme will result in a world-class pairing. Look for a good Chianti from one of the better areas of Tuscany, such as Chianti Classico or Chianti Rufina.

Arrange the pancetta slices, slightly overlapping each other, down the length of the roast. Arrange the 2 remaining rosemary sprigs on top. Tie the roast at 1-inch intervals with cotton string to give it a neat shape (see page 70). Transfer to a platter, cover with plastic wrap, and refrigerate for at least 2 and up to 24 hours. Bring to room temperature for 1 hour before roasting.

Preheat the oven to 450°F.

Place the rack of rib bones curved side down in a shallow roasting pan. Pat the roast dry with paper towels and rub with the olive oil. Place the roast on the rack and roast for 15 minutes. Remove the pan from the oven, turn the roast over, and baste with a few tablespoons of the wine. Return the roast to the oven and reduce the temperature to 350°F. Cook for 1¼ to 1½ hours longer, turning the roast and basting it with wine every 20 minutes; reserve ½ cup of wine for the sauce. The roast is done when an instant-read thermometer inserted in the center registers 145°F.

Transfer the roast to a platter and pour the pan juices into a measuring cup. If the meat on the rack of bones is still pink and you wish to serve the ribs, place on a baking sheet and return to the oven for about 15 minutes.

Meanwhile, place the roasting pan over two burners over moderate heat; when it starts to sizzle, add the reserved ½ cup wine and cook for 2 minutes, scraping up the drippings from the bottom of the pan. Add to the pan juices in the measuring cup; let the fat rise to the surface, about 5 minutes. Skim off the fat and season the sauce with salt and pepper.

Remove the strings and carve the roast into thin slices. If serving the ribs, remove the rack from the pan and cut through the ribs. Arrange the meat and ribs on a platter and serve the pan juices on the side.

in advance You can wrap and tie the pork loin up to 1 day ahead; cover and refrigerate. Bring to room temperature for 1 hour before roasting.

▼

how to tie a boneless roast Place the roast on the work surface. Beginning 1 inch from one end of the roast, start to tie the string around the roast, leaving 5 inches free at one end and the ball of string still attached to the other. Unrolling the string from the ball as you go, wind the string around the roast in a spiral fashion, leaving about 1-inch intervals between the coils of string. When you get to the other end of the roast, unroll enough string to run three times around the length of the roast. Run the end several times around the last coil of string to make a knot. Then wrap the string around the length of the roast and tie the two ends of string together to secure.

Alternatively, place the roast on the work surface. Beginning ¾ inch from one end of the roast, tie a length of string around the roast and knot it. Repeat at ¾-inch intervals, until you reach the other end.

tuscan herb salt | **makes about ¹/₄ cup** | In Tuscany, this vibrantly flavored herb salt is used to season all kinds of roasts, from pork to guinea hen. While it is best fresh, you can also let it dry out in an uncovered container—the salt will preserve the herbs' and garlic's clear flavor—to use as a versatile seasoning. I love to toss some with sautéed vegetables like green beans or potatoes. You can also vary the combination of herbs, using thyme or savory in the same way. You will need about ¼ cup herb leaves in all.

1	garlic clove
1	tablespoon kosher salt
1	small bunch fresh sage (about 30 leaves)
2	sprigs fresh rosemary

On a cutting board, mince the garlic with the salt. Place the herbs in a mound and coarsely chop them. Add the garlic salt and chop them together to make a coarse rub. Use the salt right away, or let it dry, uncovered, in a bowl for a few days.

in advance The dried salt rub can be stored indefinitely in a clean dry jar.

pork with figs and charcuterie from THE ELEMENTS OF TASTE

serves 4 | This was one of those invented-while-walking-up-and-down-the-aisles-of-the-supermarket dishes; the thought process in it is a good example of how one uses taste elements to design a dish. The hard salami and figs suggested themselves for salt and balancing sweetness. We figured the bulbiness of the onions would pull up all of the strong tastes in the wide palate of this recipe.

meat

pork

2   pounds pork loin

Kosher salt

Freshly ground white pepper

2   tablespoons grapeseed or other neutral vegetable oil

Preheat the oven to 350 degrees. Season the pork with salt and pepper. Film a roasting pan with the oil and heat over high heat until it is just about at the smoking point. Sear the pork on all sides until golden, then transfer to the oven and roast, basting frequently with pan juices, until a meat thermometer inserted in the pork indicates a temperature of 160 degrees, about 35 minutes. Remove the pork from the oven and allow it to rest for about 10 minutes. Reserve the pan juices.

topping

2   tablespoons pork pan juices (or extra virgin olive oil)

1/2   cup finely diced onions

6–8 slices Italian hard salami, julienned

1/2   cup julienned cornichons

1/2   pound fresh figs, sliced

Freshly ground white pepper

Pinch sugar

FOOD & WINE test-kitchen tips

- Rather than white pepper, we used black, which tasted fine to us.

wine recommendation   A robust wine is called for with this meaty dish. The hearty wines of the Languedoc-Roussillon region of southern France will fill the bill nicely.

71

Heat the pan juices (or oil) in a large skillet over medium-high heat. Add the onions and cook, stirring occasionally, until they are golden. Add the hard salami, cornichons, and figs, and continue sautéing for 3 minutes. Season with salt, pepper, and sugar.

plating Slice the pork in 1-inch slices and arrange on warm plates. Spoon the topping over the pork and serve.

tacos of bbq pork loin, roasted red bliss potatoes, and tomatillo–red pepper relish from BOBBY FLAY COOKS AMERICAN

serves 4 | The pork taco, in my opinion, is one of the great culinary creations of the Americas. Tender shreds of slow-cooked pork are a basic ingredient in a lot of dishes from the Texas-Mexico border, where some of my favorite food comes from. Pork, potatoes, and tomatillos are an amazing combination I discovered there. When you wrap them in corn tortillas with a red pepper salsa and a little cheese, then melt the cheese and crisp the tortilla in a hot oven or on a grill, it makes a fantastic dish. You could also sear the tacos on both sides in a hot, oiled skillet.

meat

for the pork

2   pork loins (about 1½ pounds each)

Salt and freshly ground pepper

2   cups barbecue sauce of your choice

3   cups low-sodium canned chicken stock

for the relish

2   roasted red peppers, peeled, seeded, and coarsely chopped

4   tomatillos, husked and coarsely chopped

½   red onion, finely diced

1   jalapeño, finely diced

¼   cup freshly squeezed lime juice

2   tablespoons olive oil

1   tablespoon honey

Salt and freshly ground pepper

¼   cup coarsely chopped cilantro

FOOD & WINE test-kitchen tips

- We used pork tenderloins in this recipe, and the tacos were yummy.

- We sprinkled the 3 pounds of pork with 1 teaspoon of salt and found a teaspoon was just right for the relish too.

wine recommendation This Southwestern dish calls for an all-American wine. A gutsy young Zinfandel is just the ticket.

73

for the tacos

Eight 6-inch corn tortillas

$^3/_4$ cup finely grated white cheddar cheese

$^3/_4$ cup finely grated Monterey Jack cheese

$^1/_2$ red onion, finely sliced

4   Red Bliss potatoes or other small potatoes,
    roasted or boiled until soft and sliced $^1/_2$-inch thick

$^1/_4$ cup chopped cilantro

Canola oil

1   Start the pork: Preheat the oven to 325°F. Season the pork with salt and pepper and brush with 1 cup of the barbecue sauce. Place the pork in a saucepan. Pour the stock around the pork and bring to a simmer on top of the stove. Cover and place in the oven to braise for 1 hour, or until cooked through. Remove from the cooking liquid. Bring the cooking liquid to a boil on top of the stove and reduce by half. Reserve.

2   Finish the pork: Heat a grill pan or heavy skillet until almost smoking. Place the pork in the pan, brush with the reserved barbecue sauce, and sear 2–3 minutes on each side, basting with more sauce, until a crust forms. Let rest and slice against the grain of the meat into ¼-inch slices.

3   Make the relish: Combine all the ingredients in a medium bowl. Let rest at room temperature for 30 minutes.

4   Make the tacos: Preheat the oven to 350°F. Lightly oil a sheet pan. Lay the tortillas on a flat surface. Sprinkle 1 tablespoon of each kind of cheese over each tortilla. Place a few slices of onion over the cheese, then 3–4 slices of potatoes. Dip the sliced pork into the cooking liquid to moisten, then place 3–4 slices of pork on top of the cheese. Place a little more of the cheese on top of the pork, then some of the cilantro. Fold the tortilla over and press down slightly. Brush the tops of the tortillas with some of the oil and place on the baking sheet. When all the tacos have been assembled, bake until the tortillas are lightly golden brown and the cheese has melted, 5–7 minutes. Serve topped with relish.

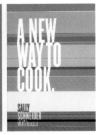

lacquered baby back ribs

from A NEW WAY TO COOK | serves 4

Cooking spareribs (a dietarily "incorrect" meat) in a foil package as a preliminary step tenderizes them while rendering out most of their fat. Then you can roast or grill them slowly, basting them with a pungent marinade until their surface is lacquered and caramelized. These ribs are as free of fat as they can possibly be.

3	tablespoons dark brown sugar
1	tablespoon Sandy's Curry Powder (next page) or commercial curry powder
1	teaspoon whole cloves
$1/2$	teaspoon cayenne pepper
$1/2$	teaspoon ground allspice
$1/2$	teaspoon kosher salt
$1/4$	teaspoon coarsely ground black pepper
$1/4$	cup plus 2 tablespoons reduced-sodium soy sauce or tamari
2	tablespoons fresh lime juice
2	tablespoons dark rum
1	tablespoon minced fresh ginger
2	garlic cloves, minced
4	racks baby back pork ribs (5 ribs per rack; $3^1/2$ to 4 pounds), trimmed of excess fat

In a large bowl, combine all the ingredients except the ribs, mixing well. Add the ribs and turn to coat. Cover and marinate for $2^1/2$ hours at room temperature. Or refrigerate for up to 12 hours; let sit at room temperature for 1 hour before roasting.

Preheat the oven to 325°F.

Remove the ribs from the marinade and brush off any cloves or pieces of ginger or garlic; reserve the marinade. Wrap each rack tightly in foil and place on a baking sheet. Roast the ribs for $1^1/2$ hours.

FOOD & WINE test-kitchen tips

- Don't worry if you run out of marinade to baste the ribs. Just use it until it's gone.

wine recommendation Côtes-du-Rhône makes an excellent match for pork, and you can find a good, inexpensive bottle in just about any wine store. If you're feeling more adventurous, seek out a close relative of Côtes-du-Rhône, a smoky Pinotage from South Africa.

Meanwhile, if you wish to grill the ribs, light a charcoal or wood fire and allow it to burn down to white-hot coals. In a small saucepan, bring the marinade to a boil over moderate heat; boil for 30 seconds.

Remove the ribs from the foil, being careful of the escaping steam, and place on a rack on a baking sheet or on the grill rack. Roast or grill, brushing the ribs with the marinade every 10 minutes, for 30 minutes. Turn the ribs over and cook, basting every 10 minutes, until the ribs are brown and glazed, about 30 minutes longer. Cut the ribs apart through the joints and serve.

in advance You can marinate the ribs up to 12 hours ahead.

meat

sandy's curry powder | makes about ¹/₃ cup | Unable to find a great commercial curry powder, talented cook and friend Sandy Gluck divined her way through an array of spices to make this curry powder, with its lovely balance of sweet pungent flavors. Use it in any recipe that calls for curry powder, or to crust panfried shrimp and scallops.

When I do stumble across a decent commercial curry powder, usually at an Indian food market or from a fine spice store, I note that invariably, the list of spices on the label begins with either coriander or cumin seeds. I have found that turmeric is usually the main ingredient in inferior curry powders. This inexpensive, rather one-dimensional spice with an appealing yellow color is often used to extend more expensive ones.

2   tablespoons coriander seeds
2   teaspoons cumin seeds
1   teaspoon black peppercorns
1¹/₂ teaspoons fennel seeds
1   teaspoon ground turmeric
1   teaspoon ground mustard
1   teaspoon ground ginger
1   teaspoon ground cinnamon

In a small heavy skillet, combine the coriander, cumin, and peppercorns and toast over moderate heat, stirring constantly, until fragrant. Remove from the heat and stir in the remaining spices.

▼

Scrape the spices into a blender container or spice grinder and blend for at least 1 minute at high speed, until you have the finest-possible powder. Let the mixture settle for about 30 seconds before removing the cover, so the fine powder does not fly into the air.

Use a dry pastry brush to press the powder through a strainer into a clean dry container. Blend and strain the larger bits again.

in advance   Store in a tightly sealed jar away from light for up to 3 months.

variation

fiery curry powder   Increase the peppercorns to 2 teaspoons and add ½ teaspoon red pepper flakes after the spices are toasted.

little pork meatballs from bari *polpette al barese* from ENOTECA

serves 6 | Italians loyally support their local businesses with pride. The Enoteca De Candia has been in operation in the Apulian city of Bari for seventy-five years. During World War II it doubled as a bomb shelter. Despite its long history, the owners have never gotten around to adding a full kitchen. This did not stop Alessandra De Candia from generously sending me many traditional Apulian recipes. These pork-and-cheese meatballs were among them. They may be served hot as a small plate, all golden and crunchy, without a sauce. Or they may be incorporated into a *ragù* to dress pasta or lasagna. I particularly like them in a tomato sauce with greens. Accompany with polenta or olive oil mashed potatoes.

1   pound ground meat, part veal and part pork or all pork

1   cup fresh bread crumbs, soaked in broth, milk, or water, then squeezed dry

$2/3$ cup grated pecorino cheese

6   tablespoons chopped fresh flat-leaf parsley

2 or 3 cloves garlic, minced

1 or 2 eggs, lightly beaten

Salt and freshly ground black pepper

Olive oil for frying

optional greens

2   pounds spinach or Swiss chard, large stems removed

2   tablespoons olive oil

$1^{1}/_{2}$ cups chopped onion

2   cloves garlic, minced

1   cup Tomato Sauce (page 81)

1   cup meat stock

1   teaspoon grated lemon zest

Salt and freshly ground black pepper

FOOD & WINE test-kitchen tips

- The easiest way to make the fresh bread crumbs for this recipe is to cut off the crusts from several slices of Italian bread (to stay with the theme, but any good bread will do) and whir the soft centers in a food processor.

- The method described in this recipe for seasoning a raw meat mixture is the professional one: cook a little bit of the meat and taste. This is more efficient if you know at least a ballpark amount, as do chefs. We used $3/4$ teaspoon salt and $1/4$ of pepper.

To make the meatballs combine the meat, bread crumbs, cheese, parsley, and garlic in a bowl. Mix in 1 egg. If the mixture seems dry, add the second egg. Season with salt and pepper. Fry a nugget of the mixture to test the seasoning. When you are happy with the flavors, form the mixture into walnut-sized balls.

Pour olive oil to the depth of ¼ inch into a large sauté pan and place over high heat. When the oil is hot, add the meatballs and fry, turning as necessary, until golden on the outside. If you are serving them plain, continue frying them until cooked through, about 10 minutes, then turn out onto a plate. If you are combining them with the greens, remove from the heat.

If serving with greens, rinse the greens well, then place in a large sauté pan with only the rinsing water clinging to the leaves. Place over medium heat and cook, turning as needed, until wilted, 3 to 5 minutes. Transfer to a colander and drain well, pressing with the back of a spoon. Chop coarsely, squeeze dry, and set aside.

Warm the olive oil in a large sauté pan over medium heat. Add the onion and garlic and sauté until tender, about 10 minutes. Add the Tomato Sauce, stock, and lemon zest and bring to a simmer. Add the browned meatballs and simmer for several minutes until cooked through. Add the cooked greens and simmer for a minute or two longer until heated through. Taste and adjust the seasoning, then serve hot or warm.

matching pointer Medium-bodied red wines with a trace of earth and adequate tannins (to balance the bitterness from the greens) are a good match. **italian wines** Rosso Conero, Nebbiolo d'Alba **alternative wines** Grenache blends (southern France, North Africa, Spain), Pinot Noir (California's central coast, Burgundy)

tomato sauce salsa di pomodoro

1 can (28 ounces) plum tomatoes, with their juices
1/2 cup tomato purée
Salt and freshly ground black pepper
2 tablespoons unsalted butter, cut into small pieces (optional)
2 tablespoons extra-virgin olive oil (optional)
Pinch of sugar
6 fresh basil leaves, chopped (optional)
1/2 cup to 3/4 cup heavy cream (optional)

Place the tomatoes and their juices in a food processor and process until finely chopped but not liquefied. Transfer to a heavy saucepan. Stir in the tomato purée and place over low heat. Bring to a simmer and cook, stirring often, until the sauce is slightly thickened, about 20 minutes. Season with salt and pepper. If desired, stir in the butter or olive oil for a smoother finish, and the sugar or basil if needed to balance the flavors. For a richer, sweeter, thinner sauce, stir in the cream.

meat

pasta gratin with leeks, sausages, and mushrooms

maccheroni al porro, salsicce, e porcini

from ENOTECA | **serves 8**

At Enoteca Cantoniere Romana in Cividale del Friuli, this wonderful dish is made with fresh porcini. That would be a considerable luxury for most of us, but fresh cultivated mushrooms augmented with some dried porcini for flavor make a satisfying pasta gratin.

- 1 pound rigatoni, penne, or other macaroni
- 7 tablespoons olive oil
- 4 large leeks, or 6 smaller leeks
- 4 tablespoons unsalted butter

Salt and freshly ground black pepper

Freshly grated nutmeg

- 1 pound sweet Italian sausages, casings removed and meat crumbled
- 1 pound fresh mushrooms, sliced
- 2 cups Classic Cream Sauce (next page)

Small handful (about $1/2$ ounce) dried porcini mushrooms, soaked in hot water to soften for 30 minutes, drained with liquid reserved and strained through a cheesecloth-lined sieve, and mushrooms chopped (optional)

- 1 cup grated Parmesan cheese

Bring a large pot filled with salted water to a boil. Add the pasta and cook until al dente; the timing will depend on the type of pasta used. Drain and toss with 2 tablespoons of the olive oil. Set aside.

Meanwhile, cut off most of the green from the leeks, and then cut the leeks in half lengthwise. Cut the halves crosswise into pieces about ¾ inch wide. Place in a deep bowl of cold water, and let the dirt settle to the bottom. Using a wire skimmer or slotted spoon, transfer to a clean bowl.

FOOD & WINE test-kitchen tips

- If you don't have the individual ramekins suggested in the recipe, use one big gratin dish, or any large ovenproof dish.

- For a nice, golden crust, bake the pasta on the top shelf of the oven at 350°.

Melt 2 tablespoons of the butter with 2 tablespoons of the olive oil in a large saucepan. Add the leeks and sauté, adding a bit of water as needed to moisten, until tender and cooked through, 10 to 15 minutes. Season with salt, pepper, and nutmeg, remove from the heat, and set aside.

Warm 1 tablespoon of the olive oil in a nonstick sauté pan over medium-high heat. Add the sausage and fry until cooked through and golden, about 5 minutes. Using a slotted spoon, transfer to a bowl and set aside.

For the fresh mushrooms, warm the remaining 2 tablespoons butter and 2 tablespoons olive oil in a large sauté pan over high heat. Add the fresh mushrooms and sauté, stirring occasionally, until they give off their liquid, about 6 minutes. Add the cream sauce and the porcini and their soaking liquid, if using. Season with salt, pepper, and nutmeg. Fold in the cooked leeks, the cooked sausage, ½ cup of the Parmesan, and the cooked pasta. Mix well.

Divide among 8 buttered ramekins. Top evenly with the remaining ½ cup Parmesan cheese. Bake until golden and bubbling, about 15 minutes. Serve at once.

matching pointer The sausage and leeks lend a rustic character to this dish and help to define the wine. The sausage will require some tannin to counterbalance its richness. The leeks demand a light, leafy element. **italian wines** Aglianico del Vulture, Salice Salentino **alternative wines** Softer Rhône blends (France, California), Cabernet Franc blends (France, California)

classic cream sauce salsa besciamella tradizionale

¼ cup unsalted butter
¼ cup all-purpose flour
2 cups milk or light cream, heated
Salt and freshly ground black pepper
Freshly grated nutmeg

Melt the butter in a saucepan over medium heat. Add the flour and cook, stirring, until it is well incorporated, about 3 minutes. Slowly stir in the hot milk or cream and cook, stirring often, until quite thick and the flour has lost all of its raw taste, about 8 minutes. Season with salt, pepper, and nutmeg and remove from the heat.

angiulino's ultimate pasta al forno with teeny meatballs

from LA BELLA CUCINA | serves 6

Angiulino's place—trattoria is too fancy a name for this simple establishment—is one of the oldest still-functioning hole-in-the-wall places in Lecce. You walk down narrow cobblestone streets with marvels of southern Italian baroque architecture on either side of you—not the overly ornate and ponderous style we think of immediately when the word *baroque* is mentioned. Here in the Salento, the baroque buildings are exuberant, yes, but it is a happy exuberance—nothing tortured or sinister about it, just fruits and flowers and decorative elements combined on the lighthearted façades carved from regional golden limestone.

Angiulino's place has the simple foods I love: steamed mussels, cooked greens, thin breaded cutlets, and, of course, his *pasta al forno*, a dish that is soul-satisfying right down to your toes. And don't forget the red wine, preferably a light, fresh red wine like the one Angiulino pours for everyone.

simple tomato sauce

- 3 tablespoons extra-virgin olive oil
- 1 medium onion, finely diced
- 1 tablespoon chopped garlic
- 1 fresh bay leaf
- 1/4 cup coarsely chopped Italian parsley
- 2 28-ounce cans imported whole peeled San Marzano plum tomatoes

Sea salt

FOOD & WINE test-kitchen tips

- The easiest way to peel a garlic clove is to put the flat side of a cleaver or large knife blade over the garlic and then crack it with a blow to the blade, using either the side of your fist or the heel of your hand. The skin will slip right off.

- Remove the bay leaf from the tomato sauce before tossing it with the pasta and other ingredients.

polpettine

1/2 pound freshly ground beef

1/2 pound freshly ground pork

About 2 cups dried country bread, soaked in water, then squeezed dry

1 egg, lightly beaten

1/4 cup grated pecorino cheese

1 garlic clove, finely chopped

1/4 cup chopped Italian parsley

Generous grindings of black pepper

assembling the dish

1 pound rigatoni, preferably artisanal

Drizzles of extra-virgin olive oil

1 pound fresh mozzarella in water, drained and coarsely shredded

1 1/2 cups grated pecorino cheese

1 cup bread crumbs

Heat the olive oil and onion in a large sauté pan over low heat until the onion is tender and transparent. Add the garlic, bay leaf, and parsley, and cook for an additional few minutes.

Add the tomatoes and their juices, first squeezing out the seeds from the tomatoes or gently scooping them out with your fingers. Season with salt. Simmer for 15 minutes or until the tomatoes break down into a sauce. Use a wooden spoon to break up the tomatoes as they cook. Taste for salt. Set aside.

Combine the ingredients for the polpettine until amalgamated. Wet your hands lightly with water. Shape the mixture into very small meatballs the size of marbles, and not any larger.

Lightly oil a baking sheet. Arrange the meatballs on the sheet, allowing space between the polpettine. Cook the meatballs under a broiler set on low for about 4 minutes, shaking the baking sheet every so often to evenly distribute the heat. Drain the meatballs on paper towels.

Heat the oven to 400 degrees. It must be very hot when the pasta goes in.

Cook the pasta in abundant salted boiling water. Drain when half cooked, about 5 minutes or so, and toss with a few drops of olive oil to prevent pasta from sticking.

Moisten the inside of a large baking dish with olive oil. The baking dish of choice is a *tiella*, a glazed ceramic vessel, one measuring 12 to 14 inches in diameter. Or use a 10 x 14-inch gratin dish.

Toss the rigatoni with the tomato sauce, polpettine, mozzarella, and 1 cup of the grated pecorino cheese. Sprinkle the top evenly with bread crumbs and the remaining grated cheese. Drizzle with a few fine threads of olive oil.

Bake uncovered for 45 minutes or until the top is golden brown. Let rest for 10 minutes, or up to 20 minutes if you can bear waiting, to allow the ingredients to adhere. Serve it forth, cut into wedges that usually fall apart very appealingly.

meat

Soffritto
Tradition & Innovation in Tuscan Cooking

Benedetta Vitali
Photographs by Gary Wolinsky

stracotto al vino rosso
stracotto with chianti from SOFFRITTO

serves 8 | This is a main course, to be accompanied by spinach, green beans, or *Puré di Patate* (see page 204).

- 1   small red onion, minced
- 1   carrot, peeled and minced
- 1   stalk celery, minced
- $^1/_3$ cup (75 ml) extra virgin olive oil
- 2   pounds (1 kg) girello (veal top round), in one piece
- 1   teaspoon all-purpose (plain) flour
- 1$^1/_2$ cups (375 ml) Chianti or other red wine
- $^1/_3$ cup (75 ml) meat stock or water
- Salt

Brown the onion, carrot, and celery in the oil in a large saucepan over medium heat just until the soffritto begins to take on a light golden color, about 5 to 10 minutes. Add the whole piece of meat and sauté together with the soffritto for 15 minutes, turning the meat gently to brown all sides. When both meat and vegetables are browned, mix in a teaspoon of flour, stirring continuously to avoid lumps. Pour in the wine and the stock and add a little salt. Turn down the heat under the pot and simmer, covered, for about 90 minutes. Turn the meat from time to time while cooking so that each part of it is submerged for a while in the liquid.

When the meat is tender to a fork, remove it from the pot, reserving the cooking juices. Slice it ¼ inch (½ cm) thick and serve piping hot, pouring abundant cooking juices over each slice.

meat

FOOD & WINE test-kitchen tips

- Red onions vary in sweetness. When we tested this recipe, the onion was quite sweet and therefore burned before the other vegetables started to color. To play it safe, you might wait to put in the onion until you add the meat.

- We found that 1½ teaspoons salt was the right amount to season the meat.

wine recommendation It is usually a good bet that the type of wine in a recipe will make a fine match for the finished dish. Chianti will be just lovely with this.

my favorite veal chops

from PRIME TIME EMERIL

makes 4 servings | When veal chops like this are served in Italy, you have the option of having the chopped arugula on top or on the side, but always with a squeeze of fresh lemon. Now, there are a couple of special directions in this recipe that will help you achieve perfect results. First, you need to pound the chops really thin, to just ¼-inch thickness, then cook them in clarified butter. This way, the chops are going to have a great flavor that just can't be reached any other way. It's definitely worth the extra effort to clarify your own butter.

Four 12-ounce bone-in veal chops

2 tablespoons plus 2 teaspoons Emeril's Original Essence or Creole Seasoning (page 93)

1 cup bleached all-purpose flour

1 cup fine dried bread crumbs

2 large eggs

1 cup milk

$\frac{1}{2}$ cup clarified butter (see Note next page)

1 bunch arugula, stemmed, washed, patted dry, and chopped (about 1$\frac{1}{2}$ cups)

4 ripe plum tomatoes (about 1$\frac{1}{4}$ pounds), cored and chopped

2 tablespoons extra-virgin olive oil

2 teaspoons fresh lemon juice

$\frac{1}{2}$ teaspoon kosher salt

$\frac{1}{4}$ teaspoon freshly ground black pepper

1 lemon, cut into 4 wedges

1 One at a time, using a thin sharp knife, cut a slit into the side of the meaty part of each chop, about 3 inches long and 1 inch deep, being careful not to cut all the way through to the bone. Gently open out the chop so the meat surface is about twice as wide as before. Place the chop between two large pieces of plastic wrap on a work surface. Using a flat meat mallet, pound the meat until ¼ inch thick.

2 Season both sides of each chop with ½ teaspoon of the Essence. Combine the flour with 1 tablespoon of the Essence in a shallow bowl. Put the bread crumbs in another shallow bowl and season with the remaining 1 tablespoon Essence. Combine the eggs and milk in another shallow bowl and whisk to blend.

3 Dredge the chops in the seasoned flour and shake off excess. Dip in the egg wash, and then coat both sides with the bread crumbs. Set on a baking sheet.

4 Heat the clarified butter in a large heavy nonstick skillet over medium-high heat. Two at a time, add the chops and cook until golden brown, about 3 minutes per side. Cut into a chop at the bone to check for doneness—they should be barely pink. Using a slotted spatula, transfer the chops to a baking sheet and keep warm in the oven while you cook the other chops.

5 Meanwhile, toss the arugula, tomatoes, olive oil, lemon juice, salt, and pepper in a large bowl.

6 Place a chop on each plate. Mound a portion of the arugula salad on top of each chop, and serve with a lemon wedge on the side.

note What makes clarified butter so great is its higher smoke point. This means you can cook meats and fish at a higher temperature than with regular butter, making it ideal for panfrying. By clarifying the butter during a slow cooking process, you're able to strain out the milk solids that burn quickly, as well as the water and salt.

To make your own clarified butter at home, just cut unsalted butter into 1-inch pieces and melt it slowly over low heat in a heavy saucepan. Remove the pan from the heat and let the melted butter stand for 5 minutes. Skim the foam from the top, and slowly pour the clarified butter into a container, discarding the milky solids in the bottom of the pan. You'll lose about one-quarter of your original butter amount during the process. Clarified butter will keep tightly covered in the refrigerator for about one month.

▼

FOOD & WINE test-kitchen tips

- The preparation of the chops sounds a little tricky, but it's actually easy. This is what we did: make a big enough cut through each chop so that you can open it up like a book, with the bone as the spine. Spread it out bone side up and pound as directed.

- If the bones in the chops are thick, the meat won't lie completely flat; it'll look more like a squat little tepee. We found that sautéing the chops on three sides, 3 minutes on each, cooked them to just the right degree of doneness and made them crisp all over. Start with the bone up, then flip to one side, then the other.

  wine recommendation The spiciness of this dish will be complemented by an aromatic Pinot Gris from the Alsace region of France.

creole seasoning | **makes about $^2/_3$ cup** | The secret to Louisiana cooking is seasoning, and every cook or chef prefers to create his or her own. Some like theirs with more heat; others prefer more herbs. Here's a recipe for making your own, which is based on my Emeril's Original Essence, now available in supermarkets and gourmet shops. If you make your own, be sure to use new herbs and spices. There's nothing worse than ingredients that have been sitting on your spice rack for years; they have no flavor. No matter which one you use—your version or mine—this is the secret ingredient that kicks everything up. Double or triple the recipe as you wish, because you'll find plenty of ways to use it.

2$^1/_2$ tablespoons paprika

2   tablespoons salt

2   tablespoons garlic powder

1   tablespoon freshly ground black pepper

1   tablespoon onion powder

1   tablespoon cayenne

1   tablespoon dried oregano

1   tablespoon dried thyme

Combine all the ingredients thoroughly in a bowl. Store in an airtight container away from light. Use within three months.

sliced steak with wine sauce
tagliata di manzo al brunello di montalcino

from ENOTECA | serves 4 to 6

Tagliata di manzo probably originated in Tuscany, home of the famous *bistecca alla fiorentina*, but it is now one of the most popular dishes throughout Italy. It may be served warm or at room temperature accompanied with classic Tuscan white beans or atop a bed of greens. Giovanni Rotti of Enoteca Giovanni in Montecatini Terme serves a fine *tagliata* marinated in a premium wine. The quality of the wine comes as no surprise, as the *signore* boasts a wine list of over five hundred labels. He takes immense pride in his Tuscan kitchen, and he's not one to skimp on ingredients. His marinated steak is seared rare and served with reduced pan juices made with an aged Brunello and aromatics. Sautéed spinach is a suitable accompaniment.

3	whole cloves
$^1/_2$	small cinnamon stick
2	bay leaves
1	clove garlic
2	fresh sage leaves
1	fresh rosemary sprig
1	whole beef fillet or thick T-bone or porterhouse steak, about $2^1/_2$ pounds
$^1/_2$	carrot, peeled and chopped
$^1/_2$	celery stalk, chopped
1	onion, chopped
$^1/_2$	bottle 7- or 8-year-old Brunello di Montalcino
2	tablespoons olive oil, plus more for sautéing

Beurre manié made from 3 tablespoons each unsalted butter
    and all-purpose flour
Salt and freshly ground black pepper

Put the cloves, cinnamon stick, bay leaves, garlic, sage, and rosemary on a square of cheesecloth, bring the corners together, and tie securely. Place the meat, carrot, celery, onion, and cheesecloth pouch in a nonreactive container, pour in the wine, turn the beef to coat evenly, cover, and refrigerate for 24 hours.

The next day, remove the beef and cheesecloth pouch and set aside. Strain the vegetables, reserving the wine and vegetables separately.

Warm the 2 tablespoons olive oil in a medium saucepan over medium heat. Add the vegetables and sauté until golden, about 15 minutes. Add the reserved wine and cheesecloth pouch, reduce the heat to low, and simmer for 1 hour.

Pass the contents of the pan through a food mill placed over a clean pan, then place the pan over low heat. Work together the butter and flour for the *beurre manié*, and gradually whisk it into the sauce to thicken. Season with salt and pepper and remove from the heat. Keep warm.

Pat the meat dry. Pour enough olive oil into a large sauté pan to form a film on the bottom and place over high heat. Sear the beef on all sides, 4 to 5 minutes on each side. It should still be quite rare but hot all the way through. Transfer to a cutting board and cut into slices about ¼ inch thick. Arrange on a platter and spoon the warm sauce over the top.

matching pointer While this dish suggests a brawny Brunello, any rich and broad-shouldered red wine will work fine. Sticking with the Sangiovese grape (the Brunello base) is recommended, although similar-styled red wines will suffice. The more cooked you like your meat, the younger your wine should be. **italian wines** Brunello di Montalcino, Super Tuscan Sangiovese and/or Cabernet-based blend **alternative wines** Rich and spicy Zinfandel, Cabernet Sauvignon

FOOD & WINE test-kitchen tips

- You can use a pinch of dried sage and ¼ teaspoon rosemary rather than the fresh herbs.

- The 8-year-old Brunello di Montalcino listed as an ingredient in this recipe costs about $70 a bottle. You may be relieved to know that a lesser wine will do very well indeed. Follow the suggestions in the Matching Pointer and choose a reasonably priced bottle.

- You can allow yourself a few hours of leeway on the meat's time in the marinade. There's nothing magical about 24 hours.

- To make the *beurre manié*, let the butter soften and then thoroughly incorporate the flour. To use the mixture, whisk pea-size pieces into the simmering sauce until it's the thickness you like. You probably won't need all of the *beurre manié*.

- If you're serving the meat at room temperature, just boil the sauce down a bit rather than thickening it with flour.

95

braised beef with salsa verde from BAYWOLF RESTAURANT COOKBOOK

serves 4 | Salsa verde is delicious with any fish, meat, or vegetable. When preparing this sauce, it is very important to chop all of the ingredients by hand; using a food processor will destroy its texture. Look for a well-marbled beef for this dish. Lean meat will tend to be dry and stringy. As with any braise, it is extremely important to cook the meat slowly and at a moderate temperature, not exceeding 350°. Cooked too hot or too quickly, the meat will dry out. This is one of the reasons I like to start meat braises two or three days in advance and let them take their time. Serve with horseradish-flavored mashed potatoes, or keep the potatoes plain and stir in a little beef bone marrow in place of some butter.

beef

3	pounds rolled beef chuck

Salt and freshly ground black pepper

2	carrots, peeled and diced
2	celery stalks, diced
1	onion, diced
4	tablespoons olive oil
4	cups beef stock, heated
6	peeled garlic cloves
2	allspice berries
1	whole clove
2	juniper berries
2	bay leaves

A few Italian parsley stems

4	thyme sprigs

sauce

2	shallots, sliced

Reserved beef trimmings

1	tablespoon reserved beef fat or olive oil
6	cups beef stock
1	thyme sprig
6	black peppercorns
1/2	bay leaf

salsa verde

Finely chopped zest and juice of 2 lemons

2   shallots, minced

2 to 4 tablespoons extra virgin olive oil

Salt and freshly ground black pepper

Finely chopped leaves of 1 thyme sprig

2   tablespoons finely chopped Italian parsley

1   tablespoon capers, rinsed and finely chopped

3   tablespoons finely chopped cornichons

to prepare the beef Two days before serving, cut the beef into 1½- by 2-inch pieces. Season with salt and pepper and refrigerate overnight. Save any meaty trim for the sauce.

The next day, preheat the oven to 325°. Sauté the carrot, celery, and onion in 2 tablespoons of the oil. Transfer to the bottom of an ovenproof pan that will just hold the beef comfortably. In the sauté pan, brown the beef in the remaining 2 tablespoons oil. Place the beef on top of the vegetables. Pour off and reserve the fat from the browning pan. Deglaze the pan with 1 cup of the beef stock and add it to the beef. Add the garlic, allspice, clove, juniper berries, bay leaves, parsley stems, and thyme and the remaining 3 cups beef stock to the pan. Cover it with parchment paper and then tightly with foil. Braise in the oven for 2 hours, then check for doneness. The meat should be fork-tender. Cool it, uncovered, in the pan. Refrigerate overnight or until serving.

▼

FOOD & WINE test-kitchen tips

- Ovens vary, as does meat, of course. When we tested this excellent recipe, the beef took half an hour beyond the minimum cooking time—2½ hours in all—to become beautifully tender. Keep testing every 15 minutes after the first 2 hours until yours is perfect.

- You may not have quarts of homemade beef stock on hand, but do use the frozen rather than canned kind for this dish. The stock is so concentrated in the sauce that anything less would be nasty.

wine recommendation This piquant preparation calls for a wine with a kick of its own. A zesty California Petite Sirah will be just right.

to prepare the beef sauce Brown the shallots and beef trim in the fat. Add 2 cups of the stock, thyme, peppercorns, and bay leaf. Simmer gently and skim the scum fastidiously. When reduced by half, add 2 more cups of stock. Continue in this fashion until all of the stock is incorporated. Reduce the sauce to a spoon-coating consistency, and then strain it through a chinois or fine strainer. Rewarm when ready to serve.

to prepare the salsa verde Put the lemon zest in a small bowl with the lemon juice and shallots. Macerate for 20 minutes, then finish with oil, salt, and pepper. Just before serving, stir in the thyme, parsley, capers, and cornichons.

to serve If you serve the beef on individual plates, instead of family style, spoon the salsa verde directly onto the meat and after you plate the beef sauce. Otherwise, you'll find oil drops floating in the beef sauce.

beef tenderloin medallions with ratatouille and anchovy–pine nut vinaigrette

from CHARLIE TROTTER'S MEAT & GAME | serves 4

The full flavor of the beef works perfectly with the lively ratatouille and is equally comple-mented by the musty, heady anchovy–pine nut vinaigrette. The ratatouille is especially explosive in flavor because all the ingredients are briefly sautéed rather than cooking them slowly together. This creates a less muddy flavor. Capers and Basil Oil provide the final whimsical, but important, flavor notes.

1	shallot, minced
1	cup plus 3 tablespoons olive oil
Pinch of saffron threads	
2	cups peeled, seeded, and chopped tomato
1	cup finely julienned Spanish onion
5	cloves garlic, minced
$1/2$	cup finely julienned red bell pepper
$1/2$	cup finely julienned yellow bell pepper
$1/2$	cup finely julienned zucchini
$1/2$	cup finely julienned yellow squash
$1/2$	cup finely julienned eggplant
2	tablespoons fresh basil chiffonade
Salt and pepper	
15	salt-packed anchovies, filleted, rinsed, and chopped
$1/4$	cup balsamic vinegar
1	red bell pepper, chopped
$1/4$	cup pine nuts, toasted
4	3-ounce beef tenderloin medallions
1	tablespoon grapeseed oil
$1/4$	cup capers, rinsed
8	teaspoons Basil Oil (page 102)

method To prepare the tomato sauce: Sweat the shallot in 1 tablespoon of the olive oil in a small sauté pan over medium-low heat for 2 minutes. Add the saffron and cook for 1 minute. Add the tomatoes and cook over medium heat for 30 minutes. Purée until smooth and pass through a fine-mesh sieve.

▼

99

To prepare the ratatouille: Sauté the onion in 2 tablespoons of the olive oil in a medium sauté pan over medium heat for 5 minutes, or until caramelized. Add the garlic and cook for 1 minute. Add the julienned red and yellow bell peppers, zucchini, yellow squash, and eggplant and cook for 5 minutes, or until the vegetables are tender. Fold the tomato sauce and basil into the vegetables and season with salt and pepper.

To prepare the vinaigrette: Purée the anchovies, balsamic vinegar, the remaining 1 cup olive oil, the chopped red bell pepper, and the pine nuts until smooth. Pass through a fine-mesh sieve and season to taste with salt and pepper. Warm the vinaigrette over medium heat for 2 to 3 minutes, or until warm.

To prepare the beef: Season the beef medallions with salt and pepper. Place the medallions in a hot sauté pan with the grapeseed oil and cook over medium heat for 4 minutes on each side, or until cooked rare. Allow the meat to rest for 3 minutes before slicing in half. Season with salt and pepper.

assembly Place some of the ratatouille in the center of each plate. Set 2 pieces of the meat over the ratatouille and sprinkle the capers around the plate. Spoon the vinaigrette and Basil Oil around the plate and top with freshly ground black pepper.

substitutions Chicken, veal, squab

wine notes While the red and yellow bell peppers in the ratatouille are well matched by a peppery Cabernet Sauvignon from Napa Valley, for the whole dish, Cabernet Franc is the better match. The herbaceous quality of Château Simard from St. Émilion in Bordeaux is a stimulating pairing with all of the other vegetable elements and the basil.

▼

meat

basil oil | **yield: 1¹/₂ cups**

$\frac{1}{2}$ cup firmly packed fresh basil leaves

$\frac{1}{2}$ cup firmly packed spinach

$\frac{1}{4}$ cup firmly packed fresh flat-leaf parsley leaves

$\frac{1}{4}$ cup olive oil

1   cup canola oil

method Blanch the basil, spinach, and parsley in boiling salted water for 45 seconds. Immediately shock in ice water and drain. Coarsely chop the mixture and squeeze out the excess water. Purée with the olive and canola oils for 3 to 4 minutes, or until bright green. Pour into a container, cover, and refrigerate for 1 day.

Strain the oil through a fine-mesh sieve and discard the solids. Refrigerate for 1 day, decant, and refrigerate until ready to use or for up to 1 week.

FOOD & WINE *test-kitchen tips*

- The only ingredients in this recipe that might be difficult for you to get are the salt-packed anchovies and the grapeseed oil. We hesitate to admit this in light of Chef Trotter's discriminating palate and demanding standards, but we substituted well-rinsed canned anchovies (30 fillets to equal 15 anchovies) and canola oil. The dish still tasted marvelous to us.

- The quickest way to cut basil into chiffonade is to stack several leaves together, roll them up loosely, and cut them crosswise into thin strips.

- For just enough of the Anchovy–Pine Nut Vinaigrette for four, make a quarter of the recipe.

- To make the tenderloin look like the picture, cut each medallion in half diagonally.

country-fried steak with white gravy

from PRIME TIME EMERIL | makes 4 servings

This Southern staple can be found in just about any restaurant in every state south of the Mason-Dixon line. It's also called "chicken-fried steak," since the steak is pounded flat, coated in crumbs, then panfried like chicken. For a real blue-plate special, round this out with some mashed potatoes, buttermilk biscuits, and southern-style cooked greens.

One $1^3/_4$- to 2-pound round steak, cut into 4 equal portions

3   tablespoons Emeril's Original Essence or Creole Seasoning (page 93)

$1/_2$ pound bacon, chopped

$1^1/_2$ cups bleached all-purpose flour

1   large egg

$2^1/_2$ cups milk

1   cup fine dried bread crumbs

$1/_2$ cup minced yellow onions

$1/_2$ teaspoon salt

$1/_4$ teaspoon freshly ground black pepper

1   Place the steak on a plastic wrap–covered work surface and cover with another piece of plastic wrap. Pound the meat to a $1/_4$-inch thickness with a meat mallet. Season both sides of the meat with $1^1/_2$ teaspoons of the Essence.

2   Fry the bacon in a large skillet until just crisp, 6 to 8 minutes. Using a slotted spoon, transfer the bacon to paper towels to drain, leaving the fat in the pan. Set the pan aside.

▼

FOOD & WINE test-kitchen tips

- We loved this, but then we're always fond of old-fashioned American food when it's done well. If "light" is your mantra, this is not the recipe for you.

- Take it easy on yourself and have the butcher pound the meat for you.

wine recommendation   A hearty dish like this calls for a bold wine. You might try a California Zinfandel that's from a good year so it will be on the full-bodied, tannic side.

3 Combine the flour with 1 tablespoon of the Essence in a large shallow bowl. Whisk the egg with ½ cup of the milk and 1½ teaspoons of the Essence in another bowl. Combine the bread crumbs and the remaining 1 tablespoon Essence in another shallow bowl or baking dish.

4 Dredge the meat in the seasoned flour, then dip in the egg wash, letting the excess drip off. Dredge the meat in the seasoned bread crumbs, coating each side evenly. Shake off any excess bread crumbs. Reserve the seasoned flour.

5 Reheat the bacon fat in the skillet over high heat until very hot but not smoking. In batches, without crowding (you may only be able to cook one portion at a time), carefully add the meat and fry until golden brown, 3 to 4 minutes on each side. Transfer to paper towels to drain.

6 Add 3 tablespoons of the reserved seasoned flour to the pan. Cook over medium-high heat, stirring constantly, for about 2 minutes, to make a light roux. Add the onions and cook, stirring often, until softened, about 4 minutes. Whisk in the remaining 2 cups milk, the salt, and pepper and bring to a boil. Reduce the heat to medium-low and simmer until the sauce is thickened and there is no raw flour taste, about 5 minutes. Stir in the bacon.

7 Serve the steaks with the hot gravy.

sichuan shredded beef with carrots and chilies *gongbao niuliu* hong kong

from MADHUR JAFFREY'S STEP-BY-STEP COOKING

serves 3 to 4 | In this spicy, slightly sweet, slightly sour dish, beef and carrot shreds are fried until they turn a bit crisp. They are then stir-fried with hot chilies and scallions and doused with a light mixture of vinegar, soy sauce, and sugar. The result is quite spectacular.

12 ounces flank steak

for the marinade

2½ teaspoons Chinese light soy sauce

1 small egg white

1 teaspoon cornstarch

1½ teaspoons sesame oil

you also need

4 medium carrots

2 garlic cloves

3 to 4 fresh hot red or green chilies

4 scallions

2½ teaspoons Chinese rice wine or dry sherry

1½ teaspoons distilled white vinegar

2½ teaspoons sugar

1 teaspoon Chinese light soy sauce

2 teaspoons Chinese dark soy sauce

Vegetable oil for deep-frying

1 teaspoon cornstarch

1 Cut the beef against the grain into wafer-thin slices, about ¹⁄₁₆ inch in width. Then stack a few slices at a time together and cut the meat into thin strips, 2½ to 3 inches long. Put the meat into a bowl. Add all the marinade ingredients and mix well, ensuring that you break up the egg white. Cover and leave to marinate for 1 to 2 hours, refrigerating if necessary.

▼

3

4

2 Peel the carrots and cut them into long thin julienne strips, the same size as the beef. Peel and finely chop the garlic. Cut the chilies lengthwise into fine strips. Cut the scallions into 3-inch lengths, then shred them lengthwise with the tip of a sharp knife into long fine strips.

Combine the rice wine, vinegar, sugar, and light and dark soy sauces in a cup. Mix well and set aside.

3 Heat a 1½-inch depth of oil in a wok on a medium heat. Add the carrots and stir-fry for 5 minutes or until slightly crisp; remove with a slotted spoon. Add the beef, turn off the heat, and stir until the pieces are separate and just turned white. To achieve this you may need a low heat. With a slotted spoon transfer the meat to a bowl. Sprinkle with the cornstarch and toss well. Increase the heat to high. Return the meat to the wok and stir-fry for 30 seconds. Turn into a strainer set over a bowl; reserve the oil. Drain the meat on paper towels.

4 Put 2 tablespoons of the reserved oil into the cleaned wok or large frying pan and set it on a high heat. When hot, add the garlic. Stir and fry for 30 seconds or until it is lightly browned. Put in the chilies, stir once, then add the scallions. Stir quickly, then add the meat strips and carrots. Stir-fry for 30 seconds, then add the rice wine sauce. Stir rapidly for about 30 seconds. Serve at once.

FOOD & WINE test-kitchen tips

- The jalapeños available now are often mild. Taste a bit of the flesh. If the flavor is almost like that of a bell pepper, include all the seeds and ribs so you get some heat into the dish.

wine recommendation   Never serve a truly great wine with a spicy dish; the subtleties of the wine will, quite literally, get lost in the sauce. Instead, look for a wine from an area that offers straightforward taste and good value. A Beaujolais-Villages will suit this dish to a tee.

calf's liver with bacon and sage

from SECOND HELPINGS FROM UNION SQUARE CAFE

serves 4 | Here's a winning recipe that combines both French and Italian flavors to great effect. Soaking the liver in milk for an hour tenderizes it. Crisp bacon, sweet onions, and sage are the key ingredients in this creamy sauce, which also works nicely with veal chops or veal scaloppine.

4   (4-ounce) slices calf's liver

Milk for soaking

$^1/_2$ cup all-purpose flour

Kosher salt

Freshly ground black pepper

2   tablespoons olive oil

4   ounces bacon, cut into $^1/_4$-inch-thick strips

2   cups sliced onion

2   tablespoons drained capers

2   teaspoons sliced fresh sage

$^1/_4$ cup white wine

1   cup brown veal stock or store-bought veal demi-glace

$^1/_4$ cup heavy cream

2   tablespoons Dijon mustard

1   Place the liver in a bowl and add enough milk to cover. Refrigerate for 1 hour.

2   Preheat the oven to 200 degrees F.

3   Pour the flour onto a dinner plate. Sprinkle the liver slices with salt and pepper and dredge in the flour. Shake off the excess.

4   In a large skillet, heat the oil over medium-high heat. Sauté the liver until golden brown, about 2 minutes on each side for medium-rare. Transfer the cooked liver to a serving platter, cover loosely, and keep warm in the oven while you make the sauce.

FOOD & WINE test-kitchen tips

- We thought store-bought veal or chicken stock worked fine in this wonderful recipe for liver lovers.

- If fresh sage isn't available, substitute about $^3/_4$ teaspoon crumbled dried sage leaves or $^1/_2$ teaspoon rubbed dried sage.

5 Discard the oil from the skillet and place over medium-high heat. Add the bacon and cook 2 minutes. Add the onion and cook until the slices are lightly browned and tender but still have body, about 5 minutes. Stir in the capers and sage. Pour in the wine and reduce until almost dry. Add the stock and reduce by two-thirds. Add the cream, mustard, $\frac{1}{2}$ teaspoon of salt, and $\frac{1}{4}$ teaspoon of pepper. Bring the sauce to a boil and reduce until thick enough to coat the back of a spoon. Spoon the sauce over the liver and serve immediately.

wine suggestions A rich, buttery chardonnay would suit this dish if you're in the mood for white, or, alternatively, go for a heady, smoky red like Châteauneuf-du-Pape, Australian shiraz, or Rioja.

meat

crispy lamb chops
braciolette croccante di agnello

from ITALIAN HOLIDAY COOKING | serves 4

At the Colle Picchioni farm and winery, olives, persimmon, and other fruit trees and rows of grapevines grow in profusion. There Paola Di Mauro and her son, Armando, make outstanding white and red wines under the Colle Picchioni label.

Paola prepared a multicourse feast when we visited her. We began with big platters of hand-made agnolotti stuffed with a mix of ground beef, pork, sausage, veal, and chicken, tossed with a bright bouquet of buttery carrots, cherry tomatoes, bell peppers, and tasty zucchini from her garden.

Next came crunchy, crispy lamb chops. We started eating them with knives and forks, then switched to fingers so we could get to every bit of meat on the bones. The meal ended with tender biscotti flavored with white wine.

16 thin rib lamb chops
2   large eggs, beaten
Salt and freshly ground black pepper
About 1½ cups dry bread crumbs, preferably homemade (see next page)
Olive oil for frying
Lemon wedges, optional

1 Trim the fat from the chops. Place them on a cutting board and pound the meat gently to about a ½-inch thickness.

2 In a shallow bowl, beat the eggs with salt and pepper to taste. Spread the bread crumbs on a plate.

FOOD & WINE test-kitchen tips

- Since the salt and pepper in the egg coating is the only seasoning the lamb chops get, we were generous: 1 teaspoon salt and ½ teaspoon pepper.

- You can add a few tablespoons of chopped fresh herbs to the bread crumb mixture if you like. Rosemary is especially good.

3 Pour about ⅓ inch of oil into a deep skillet. Heat until a bit of the egg mixture sizzles and cooks quickly when dropped into the pan. Dip a chop in the eggs, then dredge quickly in the bread crumbs, patting them on so they adhere well. Carefully place the chop in the hot oil. Repeat with just enough chops to fit comfortably in a single layer in the pan. Cook for 3 to 4 minutes per side, turning once, until browned and crisp.

4 Drain the chops on paper towels. Keep warm in a low oven while you fry the remainder. Serve hot, with lemon wedges, if desired.

wine match Vigna del Vassalo, Colle Picchioni

bread crumbs Homemade bread crumbs are easy to make from leftover slices of Italian or French bread. Do not use sliced white bread—it is soft and spongy and contains sugar and other ingredients you don't want.

Lay the slices on a baking sheet and toast them in a low oven until very dry. Let cool, break up, then grind the slices in a food processor. Store the crumbs in a tightly sealed plastic bag in the refrigerator or freezer.

agnello in fricassea
lamb with egg-lemon sauce from SOFFRITTO

serves 4 | In this recipe the base ingredient is lamb, but it could be rabbit, chicken, chunks of veal, or even boiled beef. Serve as a main course accompanied by sautéed artichokes or asparagus.

½ cup (125 ml) extra virgin olive oil

2 pounds (1 kg) lamb shoulder, cut in 1-inch (2-cm) cubes

3 or 4 leaves sage

Leaves from 1 sprig of rosemary

2 cloves garlic, coarsely chopped

½ cup (125 ml) dry white wine

Salt

2 cups (500 ml) water

2 egg yolks

Juice of 2 lemons

Freshly ground black pepper, for serving

Choose a fairly wide, heavy cast-aluminum pot that can accommodate all the meat in a single layer. Heat the oil over medium heat until it begins to bubble, and add the lamb. Brown for about 20 minutes, turning the pieces so they brown on all sides. When the browning is nearly complete, add the sage, rosemary, and garlic. Keep stirring, taking care that the garlic doesn't burn. Pour in the wine, turn the heat to high, and let the wine evaporate almost completely. Add some salt and the water, reduce the heat to low, cover, and cook for another 45 minutes. Frequently check the level of the liquid and stir with a wooden spoon, adding more hot water only as necessary so the lamb does not dry out. Toward the end of the cooking, check the lamb with a fork; it should be tender. The juice that remains should not be liquid, but thick.

Right before you are ready to serve the lamb, gently combine the egg yolks and lemon juice in a bowl. Take the pot with the lamb off the stove and stirring continuously with a wooden spoon, pour in the egg and lemon. Keep stirring until a smooth, creamy sauce has formed. If you do not keep stirring, or if you leave the pot on the stove, you will have an omelet.

After you add the egg and lemon, the lamb cannot be reheated, so finish the *fricassea* at the very moment before serving. Serve hot, with pepper at the table.

FOOD & WINE test-kitchen tips

- This wonderful sauce is quite tangy—great with the rich lamb. Still, you may want to adjust the lemon juice to your own taste. Two lemons will give you 2 to 4 tablespoons juice. Start with 2 and add more if you like.

- The lamb can be made days ahead of time as long as you wait to finish the sauce until just before serving.

wine recommendation   An earthy Spanish Rioja will be a perfect match for this succulent lamb. For a special treat, look for an older bottle, which will be marked "Reserva" or "Gran Reserva."

fish & shellfish

filletti di sogliole fritti
fried fillets of sole with lemon and garlic

from SOFFRITTO | serves 6

This is a very simple dish, if the difficulty of filleting the sole is excluded—a task best left to your trusted fishmonger. Mediterranean sole is the ideal fish for this preparation. Of the several varieties of sole (really flounder) available in North America, several are too flaky to fry up well. Ask your fishmonger for a lean, dense-fleshed sole, like English sole, petrale sole, or lemon sole, for the best results. This main dish is very agreeably accompanied by spinach blanched in salted boiling water and seasoned simply with good olive oil and a little lemon.

12   fillets of sole

Salt

Freshly ground black pepper

2   cloves garlic, minced

2   tablespoons minced flat-leaf parsley

2 or 3 tablespoons all-purpose (plain) flour

1   egg

1/3   cup (30 g) dried bread crumbs

About 2 cups (500 ml) extra virgin olive oil

1   teaspoon (5 ml) freshly squeezed lemon juice

Spread the fillets on a cutting board and season them with salt, a little pepper, and pinches of the garlic and parsley. Starting from the top, roll up the fillets as tightly as you can, then roll them in the flour and set them aside for a moment. Beat the egg with a pinch of salt. Dip the rolled-up fillets in the egg, then roll them in the bread crumbs.

Choose a frying pan wide enough to accommodate all the fillets at once, and cover the bottom with 1 inch (2 cm) of oil. Heat over a high flame. The oil is ready when a bread crumb dropped in it sizzles. Fry the fillets for about 3 minutes, then turn them over and fry for another 2 to 3 minutes on the other side. The fillets should be browned well on both sides. Remove the fillets from the oil and drain them very briefly on absorbent paper, then serve immediately. Once fried, the fillets should be eaten very hot, sprinkled with a few drops of lemon juice.

FOOD & WINE test-kitchen tips

- In this recipe, the quantities of flour, egg, and bread crumbs to coat the sole may seem small. Don't be tempted to use more; stick to the conservative amounts for an ideally thin and crisp crust.

wine recommendation In order not to overwhelm the delicate taste of the sole, a light, somewhat neutral wine is best. Ask your wine merchant to recommend a good-quality Orvieto.

parmigiano-crusted grouper from SECOND HELPINGS
FROM UNION SQUARE CAFE

serves 4 | Though the combination of grouper and Parmigiano-Reggiano may seem a bit out of the ordinary, the two get along just fine here, with the cheese adding a buttery, nutty flavor, as well as a nice crunchy crust to the fish fillets. To preserve the browned crust, the warm red-pepper vinaigrette gets spooned around the grouper, providing a sweet-and-tart counterpoint to the fish. Serve with mashed or fried potatoes and some sautéed spinach or red chard.

red-pepper vinaigrette

2	medium red bell peppers
1	small yellow bell pepper
1	small tomato, cored and roughly chopped
$1/4$	cup sliced shallots and 2 tablespoons minced shallots (about 4 large shallots)
2	tablespoons sliced garlic
1	sprig fresh thyme, plus 1 teaspoon fresh thyme leaves
1	cup white wine
$1/4$	cup red wine vinegar
1	tablespoon tomato paste
1	cup Fish Stock (page 122), reduced to $1/4$ cup
$1/4$	cup plus 1 tablespoon extra-virgin olive oil

Kosher salt

Freshly ground black pepper

parmigiano-crusted grouper

1	cup panko (or fresh bread crumbs)
$1/2$	cup grated Parmigiano-Reggiano

Kosher salt

Freshly ground black pepper

$1^1/2$	tablespoons butter, melted
4	(6-ounce) skinless grouper fillets (or red snapper or striped bass)
2	tablespoons olive oil

1 Begin the vinaigrette: Core and seed the red and yellow bell peppers. Finely dice 2 tablespoons each of the red and yellow peppers and reserve. Coarsely chop all the remaining pepper.

2 Combine the coarsely chopped pepper in a 2-quart saucepan with the tomato, sliced shallots, garlic, thyme sprig, white wine, vinegar, and tomato paste. Bring to a simmer over medium-low heat and reduce, stirring occasionally until almost dry. Transfer the cooked mixture to a food mill and puree into a large bowl.

3 Wipe out the saucepan and return the puree to the pan. Add the reduced fish stock, bring to a simmer, and cook until the puree is thickened and reduced to about 1 cup. Transfer the puree to a large bowl and make the vinaigrette by whisking in ¼ cup of the extra-virgin olive oil, ¾ teaspoon of salt and ⅛ teaspoon of pepper.

4 Heat the remaining 1 tablespoon of olive oil in a small skillet over medium heat. Add the minced shallot, diced red and yellow peppers, thyme leaves, ½ teaspoon of salt, and ⅛ teaspoon of pepper. Cook, stirring, just until the vegetables become slightly tender, 1 to 2 minutes. Add the mixture to the bowl with the red pepper vinaigrette. Set aside.

5 Preheat the oven to 450 degrees F.

6 To prepare the fish, process the panko in a food processor until it is quite fine. Transfer the bread crumbs to a bowl, and stir in the Parmigiano, ½ teaspoon of salt, ⅛ teaspoon of pepper, and the melted butter.

▼

FOOD & WINE test-kitchen tips

- The most time-consuming part of this recipe is the red-pepper vinaigrette. If you don't have time for it, skip it. The moist fish with its crisp crust is good enough to stand very well on its own.

- An ovenproof nonstick frying pan or an old-fashioned cast-iron skillet is ideal here to ensure that the crust doesn't stick to the pan.

7 Sprinkle the fillets all over with 1 teaspoon of salt and ¼ teaspoon of pepper. In an ovenproof skillet large enough to hold the fillets in one layer, heat the olive oil over medium-high heat. Add the fillets, skinned sides up, and cook until golden brown, about 3 minutes. Remove from the heat, turn over the fillets, and generously coat the browned sides with the cheese and bread-crumb mixture, pressing the breading onto the fish. Place the skillet in the oven and bake until the fish is cooked through and the breading is golden brown, about 5 minutes. (If the breading hasn't browned sufficiently, place under the broiler for 1 to 2 minutes.) While the fish cooks, gently reheat the vinaigrette; do not let it boil. Transfer the fish to a platter or individual plates, spoon the warm vinaigrette around the fish, and serve.

wine suggestions This versatile dish could be matched with a lively and fruity white like verdicchio or Vernaccia di San Gimignano, with a well-made rosé, or a red, such as Sangiovese di Romagna or Teroldego Rotaliano.

fish stock | makes 3¹/₂ cups | For a brilliant and flavorful fish stock, rinse the bones and heads well to remove any blood or impurities. If you are using fish heads, be sure to have the gills removed. A word of caution: never cook the stock beyond a barely perceptible simmer, to prevent it from becoming murky and unappealing.

1 tablespoon olive oil

1 cup sliced onions

1 cup well-rinsed sliced leeks (white and light green parts only)

¹/₂ cup chopped celery

1 fresh thyme sprig

3 fresh parsley sprigs

1 small bay leaf

1 teaspoon whole black peppercorns

1 pound fish bones from white-fleshed fish (such as flounder, sole, bass, or snapper), cleaned and chopped

¹/₂ cup white wine

4 cups cold water

1   Heat the olive oil over medium heat in a 3-quart stockpot or saucepan. Add the vegetables, herbs, and peppercorns and cook over medium heat, stirring frequently, until softened, about 10 minutes.

2   Raise the heat to high, add the fish bones, and stir well for 3 to 4 minutes. Add the white wine and reduce by boiling for an additional 3 to 4 minutes.

3   Add the cold water, lower the heat to medium, and slowly bring the stock to a boil. Skim the surface with a ladle to remove any foam that rises. Lower the heat some more and simmer very slowly for 45 minutes.

4   Strain the stock through a fine-mesh or cheesecloth-lined strainer and chill over ice. Refrigerate for up to 4 days, or freeze for future use.

fish & shellfish

fantastic fish pie

from THE NAKED CHEF TAKES OFF | serves 6

The whole fish pie thing is one of the most homely and comforting dinners I can think of. This is a cracking recipe which does it for me.

5   large potatoes, peeled and diced into 1-inch squares

Salt and freshly ground black pepper

2   large eggs

2   large handfuls of fresh spinach

1   onion, finely chopped

1   carrot, halved and finely chopped

Extra-virgin olive oil

Approximately $1\frac{1}{3}$ cups heavy cream

2   good handfuls of grated sharp Cheddar or Parmesan cheese

Juice of 1 lemon

1   heaped teaspoon English mustard

1   large handful of flat-leaf parsley, finely chopped

1   lb haddock or cod fillet, skin removed, pin-boned and sliced into strips

Fresh nutmeg (optional)

Preheat the oven to 450°F. Put the potatoes into salted boiling water and bring back to a boil for 2 minutes. Carefully add the eggs to the pan and cook for a further 8 minutes, until hard-boiled, by which time the potatoes should also be cooked. At the same time, steam the spinach in a colander above the pan. This will take only a minute. When the spinach is done, remove from the colander and gently squeeze out any excess moisture. Then drain the potatoes in the colander. Remove the eggs, cool under cold water, then peel and quarter them. Place to one side.

In a separate pan slowly fry the onion and carrot in a little olive oil for about 5 minutes, then add the cream and bring just to the boil. Remove from the heat and add the cheese, lemon juice, mustard and parsley. Put the spinach, fish and eggs into an appropriately sized earthenware dish and mix together, pouring over the creamy vegetable sauce. The cooked potatoes should be drained and mashed—add a bit of olive oil, salt, pepper and a touch of grated nutmeg if you like. Spread on top of the fish. Don't bother piping it to make it look pretty—it's a homely hearty thing. Place in the oven for about 25–30 minutes until the potatoes are golden. Serve with some nice peas or greens, not forgetting your baked beans and ketchup. Tacky but tasty and that's what I like.

FOOD & WINE test-kitchen tips

- English mustard is HOT. If you're substituting for it, you might want to add some dry mustard to the heaping teaspoon of prepared in order to get the same effect.

- Taste the sauce before pouring it over the spinach, fish, and eggs. We found it needed about $^{3}/_{4}$ teaspoon salt.

wine recommendation   Fish in a creamy sauce calls for a medium-bodied wine with sprightly acidity. Look for a wine from the Sauvignon Blanc grape, such as a Pouilly-Fumé from the Loire or an inexpensive white Bordeaux.

monkfish scarpariello

from SECOND HELPINGS FROM UNION SQUARE CAFE

serves 4 | This is Union Square Cafe's variation on *pollo scarpariello* (chicken "shoe-maker's style"), long a fixture on the menus of New York's Neapolitan Italian restaurants. In our recipe we've exchanged the more traditional chicken for monkfish, but have retained the tangle of sweet peppers, fennel sausage, and mushrooms. Monkfish is a lean, meaty fish that works particularly well here since it can withstand a good sauté without toughening in texture. A big bowl of steamed broccoli or sautéed broccoli rabe and a platter of fried potatoes would make terrific accompaniments.

1   small red bell pepper

1   small yellow bell pepper

¼   cup olive oil

8   pieces monkfish, 1½ to 2 inches thick, cut across the bone
     and trimmed of all dark skin (about 2 pounds total weight)

Kosher salt

Freshly ground black pepper

6   ounces fresh sweet fennel sausage, cut on the diagonal into 16 thin slices

2   cups cleaned and thinly sliced white or cremini mushrooms

1   tablespoon plus 1 teaspoon all-purpose flour

1   tablespoon plus 1 teaspoon red wine vinegar (preferably Italian)

1½   cups Chicken Stock (page 161)

½   cup homemade or good-quality store-bought tomato sauce

1   heaping tablespoon chopped fresh parsley

1 Roast and slice the peppers: spear the peppers with a kitchen fork or skewer and hold them over an open flame until charred all over. Place the charred peppers in a paper bag or in a covered container until they are cool enough to handle. (This step facilitates removing the skin.) Rub off the skins (never run them under water, which washes away the flavorful oils), cut the peppers in half lengthwise, and discard the stems and seeds. Cut the pepper halves into ¼-inch-wide strips and set aside.

2 Heat the oil in a large skillet over medium-high heat. Sprinkle the monkfish with 1½ teaspoons of salt and ½ teaspoon of pepper and cook until lightly browned, about 2 minutes on each side. Transfer the fish to a plate and reserve.

3 Add the sausage to the skillet and cook until browned on both sides, about 2 minutes. (Reduce the heat as needed to keep the skillet from burning.) Toss in the mushrooms and cook along with the sausage, stirring until softened, about 2 minutes. Add the peppers and stir in the flour. Cook for 1 minute, stir in the vinegar, stock, and tomato sauce and bring to a simmer, scraping the bottom of the pan to deglaze. Season with ½ teaspoon of salt and a pinch of pepper.

4 Return the fish to the skillet along with any juices that have accumulated on the plate. Cover the skillet and simmer gently, basting the fish occasionally, until it is just cooked through, 8 to 10 minutes. Transfer the monkfish to a warm serving platter. Return the skillet to the heat and reduce the liquid until it thickens to a sauce consistency, about 1 to 2 minutes. Taste and adjust the seasoning. Spoon the sauce, mushrooms, peppers, and sausage over the fish, sprinkle with the chopped parsley, and serve immediately.

wine suggestions Though a nice, crisp white would work, here's a good spot to break a rule and choose red wine with fish. If you're so inclined, try a Barbera d'Alba, Dolcetto d'Alba, or a Chianti Classico—any of which would lend a note of rich juiciness to the dish.

FOOD & WINE test-kitchen tips

- Although the combination of red and yellow peppers in this recipe looks pretty, you can use just 1 large red pepper if you like.

- To save time, you can use both store-bought tomato sauce and chicken stock here. The results are still wonderful.

seafood "meatballs"

polpette di pesce from BIBA'S TASTE OF ITALY

serves 4 as an entrée, 6 as an appetizer | *Polpette* (meatballs), made with meat, seafood, or vegetables, have been a staple of *la buona cucina casalinga*, good home cooking, from the time when necessity turned leftover ingredients into savory morsels. Today now that Italy has become quite affluent, these savory dishes are almost forgotten. However, in Rimini, at Quattro Colonne, an unpretentious restaurant on the pier that serves very good food, I had a plate of golden, crisp seafood *polpette* that brought back happy memories of my childhood.

3	large eggs
2	cups plus 2 to 3 tablespoons fine dried bread crumbs
	2 to 3 tablespoons freshly grated Parmigiano-Reggiano
1/3	cup chopped flat-leaf parsley
1	small garlic clove, finely minced
3	tablespoons extra virgin olive oil
1	pound firm-fleshed fish fillets, such as sturgeon, monkfish, or halibut

Salt and freshly ground black pepper to taste

Olive oil for frying

Lemon wedges

Beat 1 of the eggs in a medium bowl. Add 2 tablespoons of the bread crumbs, the Parmigiano, parsley, garlic, and oil and mix well.

Chop the fish very fine, preferably by hand, or in a food processor. If using a food processor, pulse the machine until the fish is chopped to a granular consistency; do not puree. Add the fish to the bowl, season with salt and pepper, and mix with a rubber spatula until thoroughly blended. The mixture should be soft and a bit moist, but not wet. Mix in an additional 1 tablespoon bread crumbs, if needed. (The mixture can be prepared several hours ahead. Refrigerate tightly covered with plastic wrap.)

Line a baking sheet with parchment or wax paper. Spread the remaining 2 cups bread crumbs on a sheet of aluminum foil. Lightly beat the remaining 2 eggs in a shallow bowl. Divide the fish mixture into 12 equal parts and shape each one into a ball. Dip the balls in the eggs and roll each one in the bread crumbs, flatten it lightly with the palms of your hands, and place on the baking sheet. Refrigerate the *polpette*, uncovered, for about 1 hour.

Heat 1 inch of oil in a medium heavy skillet over medium-high heat. When the oil is quite hot, lower a few *polpette* at a time into the oil with a slotted spoon and cook until one side has a light golden crust, 1 to 2 minutes. Turn them gently and cook the other side until golden brown. Remove with a slotted spoon and place on towels to drain. Serve hot, with lemon wedges.

seafood polpettine By shaping the seafood mixture into very small balls, you will have delicious, crunchy *polpettine* to serve before a meal. Shape heaping teaspoons of the mixture into small balls and dip them into the eggs and roll in the bread crumbs. Fry until golden on all sides. Insert a wooden tooth pick into each ball, place on a large platter, and let your guests help themselves.

FOOD & WINE test-kitchen tips

- So the *polpette* don't absorb too much oil, it's best if your oil is at least 350°. Be sure not to let it get above 400°, though, or they'll burn.

wine recommendation A wine with high acidity and a pronounced flavor profile of its own will be your best bet to stand up to the assertive flavor of fried fish. Try a tangy Sauvignon Blanc from New Zealand or South Africa.

thin swordfish steaks
the italian way from LA BELLA CUCINA

serves 6 | In all my travels in Italy, I don't believe I've seen swordfish sliced any thicker than about ½ inch. And for good reason. Swordfish dries out easily when overcooked. A thicker steak requires much more time on the stove. By the time the inner flesh is cooked properly, the outside has hardened. Follow this recipe and you'll never have to worry about overcooking swordfish again.

Find a purveyor of superior swordfish. I've had a few bad experiences lately with swordfish that was strangely tough and stringy, truly *schifoso*—quite disgusting.

2 pounds fresh swordfish steaks sliced no thicker than ½ inch
½ cup bread crumbs made from dried country bread
¼ cup chopped Italian parsley
1 small garlic clove, finely chopped
Sea salt
3 tablespoons extra-virgin olive oil plus extra for frying
Thick lemon wedges

Drain the swordfish well.

Stir together the bread crumbs, parsley, garlic, and sea salt on a plate.

Place 3 tablespoons of olive oil in a bowl. Moisten each steak on both sides with a brush dipped in the oil. Lightly sprinkle each side with the bread crumb mixture, gently patting it in so it adheres.

Pour in enough oil to cover the bottom of a large sauté pan and heat it over medium heat.

Cook the swordfish steaks over medium-low heat for about 2 to 3 minutes on each side. Transfer to a platter and season with a sprinkling of salt.

Serve with lemon wedges.

FOOD & WINE test-kitchen tips

- You'll need about 1 teaspoon of salt in the bread crumb mixture.

wine recommendation A full-flavored fish such as swordfish can take on an assertive white. An Australian Semillon or a South African Chardonnay will work wonders here.

miso-sake–glazed fish fillets and steaks

from A NEW WAY TO COOK

serves 4 | Many years ago, I tasted a spectacular grilled ling cod that had been marinated in sake kasu, the dregs left from the fermentation of sake, the Japanese rice wine. The marinade both cured the flesh slightly and permeated it with a faintly sweet flavor. Grilling caramelized and glazed the surface. Kasu is very difficult to find but, happily, a combination of sake, mirin, and white miso produces a similar effect.

This marinade is spectacular with fatty or oily fish such as salmon, black cod, and bluefish as well as Chilean sea bass. White miso, a paste made of fermented soybeans, is golden in color and has a sweet, mellow flavor. Mirin is sweet Japanese rice wine. Both are available at health food stores and Asian markets.

You need to marinate the fish for at least 12 hours, so plan ahead.

miso-sake glaze

1   cup sweet white miso paste

3 to 4 tablespoons dark brown sugar

$^{1}/_{4}$ cup sake

$^{1}/_{4}$ cup mirin (Japanese rice wine) or medium-dry sherry

Four 6-ounce fish steaks or fillets, such as salmon, sea bass,
      yellowtail, Chilean sea bass, black cod, or very fresh bluefish

1   teaspoon olive oil

To make the glaze, combine all the ingredients in a medium saucepan and bring to a simmer over moderate heat. Reduce the heat to low and cook for 5 minutes. Set aside to cool.

▼

FOOD & WINE test-kitchen tips

- We used salmon fillets to test this recipe and left the skin on. It got nice and crisp under the broiler.

wine recommendation   The sweet glaze here calls for a wine that has some residual sweetness of its own. Look for a Riesling labeled "Kabinett" or "Spätlese" from the Mosel region of Germany.

fish & shellfish

Red miso and sweet
white miso pastes

Spread one third of the glaze over the bottom of a glass baking dish. Arrange the fish in the dish and spread the remaining glaze over the fillets or steaks to coat them completely. Cover with plastic wrap and refrigerate for at least 12 hours, but no longer than 24 hours. Bring the fish to room temperature 30 minutes before cooking.

To cook the fish, prepare a fire in a grill or preheat the broiler.

Scrape the glaze from the fish and discard. Pat the fish dry with paper towels and brush lightly with the olive oil. Grill or broil 3 inches from the heat for 3 to 4 minutes. Turn and cook for 2 to 3 minutes longer, or until you feel no resistance when you insert a kitchen fork into the fish. Serve immediately.

in advance You can prepare the glaze up to 2 months ahead and refrigerate it. The fish must be marinated for at least 12 hours, or for as long as 24 hours.

fish & shellfish

salmone marinato freddo

cold poached salmon **from DA SILVANO COOKBOOK**

serves 4 | Italians are very resourceful people when it comes to food, and I'm proud to say I'm no different. I made up this recipe when I showed up to stay for the night at a house in Stony Point, Long Island, and found that the gas had been shut off. I found some wood and a pot, started a fire, and made this dish.

Fine sea salt

1   large carrot, peeled and cut into $^1/_8$-inch/0.25-cm rounds

1   medium red onion, peeled and quartered

1   celery stalk, cut into 3 large pieces

4   skin-on salmon fillets (about 8 oz/225g each)

8   cherry tomatoes, halved

$^1/_4$ cup/55ml Pesto, without cheese (next page)

$^1/_2$ cup/110ml Vinaigrette Modo Mio (page 136)

Bring a large pot of salted water to a boil over high heat. Add the carrot, onion, and celery, then carefully lower the salmon fillets into the pot, one at a time. Lower the heat and cook at a simmer until the salmon is cooked through but still firm, 5 to 7 minutes, depending on the thickness of the fillets. (If you prefer your fish rare, cook it a bit less.) If necessary, remove a fillet and cut into it with a paring knife to check for doneness. Keep in mind that it will continue to cook a bit by the retained heat after you take it out of the water.

Carefully remove the salmon fillets from the water and set aside to cool. Remove and discard the celery and onion. Drain the remaining liquid in a colander and refresh the carrots under gently running cold water. Cover the salmon and carrots separately and refrigerate them for at least 1 hour or up to 4 hours. Place 4 dinner plates in the refrigerator at the same time so they'll be chilled when you're ready to serve.

FOOD & WINE test-kitchen tips

- It's important to use skin-on fillets, as called for in the recipe, even though you remove the skin before serving. Without it, the fish would fall to pieces.

- Since both the pesto and the vinaigrette in this recipe can be made days before using, we tried poaching the salmon ahead too. It lasted beautifully overnight. Combine the pesto and the vinaigrette and sauce the fish with the mixture just before serving. This recipe makes an ideal summer dinner-party dish.

When ready to serve, remove the skin from each salmon fillet and cut each fillet into 4 equal portions. Place the pieces of 1 fillet in the center of each of the 4 chilled dinner plates, skinned-side down. Surround the fillets with the cherry tomato halves and carrot rounds. Pour the pesto and vinaigrette into a mixing bowl and stir them together. Drizzle some of the mixture over each portion of salmon and serve immediately, while still cold.

wine suggestion   Sauvignon, "Graf de Latour"–Villa Russiz

pesto basil pesto | **makes about 1 cup/225g** | A lot of people romanticize pesto and think about tossing it in the pan with freshly cooked pasta. But you should never do that—it will turn the basil in the pesto black. Always mix pesto with hot pasta in a bowl.

Because I use pesto with the preceding salmon recipe, I separate the cheese out in this recipe. That way, you can add the cheese only if you want or need it for a given purpose.

4   cups/225g (tightly packed) basil leaves
1   cup/140g pine nuts
1   clove garlic, smashed and peeled
1   cup/225ml olive oil
Fine sea salt
Freshly ground black pepper
About $^{1}/_{2}$ cup/55g freshly grated Parmigiano-Reggiano

Place the basil, pine nuts, and garlic in a food processor. With the motor running, add the olive oil in a thin stream, then season with salt and pepper. Continue to process until a pourable liquid is formed.

Keep pesto in an airtight container in the refrigerator for up to 1 week. Pour a little film of olive oil over it to keep it as fresh as possible.

Add the cheese (about 1 tablespoon per person) just before serving or using.

▼

vinaigrette modo mio vinaigrette my way | **makes about 2 cups/^{1}/2 litre**

This is a delicious, all-purpose salad dressing. The key is the soybean oil (a.k.a. vegetable oil), which is much lighter than olive oil.

^{1}/4   cup/55ml red wine vinegar

1^3/4 cups/400ml soybean oil

1   small garlic clove, minced

Pinch fine sea salt

Pinch freshly ground black pepper

Pinch dry mustard, preferably Colman's English Mustard

Place all the ingredients in a ceramic or stainless steel bowl. Whisk together well. Use right away or refrigerate in an airtight container for up to 3 days.

pan roasted salmon with aromatic salted herbs

from THE ELEMENTS OF TASTE

serves 4 | We wanted to simplify the long process of a traditional gravlax, by making a fresh herb and salt topping with gravlax ingredients. The tastes would be the same, but rather than infusing the salmon, the taste of the topping remains distinct and lets the nice texture of cooked salmon come out while still preserving the oomph of the spices and salt.

herbs

2 tablespoons thinly sliced chives

$^1/_2$ cup finely chopped parsley

$^1/_3$ cup finely chopped mint

$^1/_3$ cup finely chopped dill

Combine the herbs in a large bowl.

salt and spice mix

$1^1/_2$ tablespoons coarse salt

$^1/_8$ teaspoon cayenne pepper

$^1/_8$ teaspoon ground cardamom

$^1/_2$ teaspoon ground nutmeg

$^1/_2$ teaspoon coarse ground white pepper

In a separate bowl, combine the salt and spices.

salmon

2 tablespoons peanut or other neutral vegetable oil

4 6-ounce salmon fillets, each about 1 to $1^1/_2$ inches thick, skin on

Kosher salt

Finely ground white pepper

Cayenne pepper

2 tablespoons butter

▼

FOOD & WINE test-kitchen tips

- If you want just enough of the salt and spice mix for this recipe, cut the quantities in half.

wine recommendation With this elegant dish, look for a white Burgundy with the name of the village on the label. For value, try one of the lesser-known areas such as St-Aubin or Rully.

Preheat the oven to 225 degrees. Heat the oil in a large ovenproof skillet over medium-low heat. Add the salmon, skin side down, and cook until crispy, about 2 minutes. Season to taste with salt, pepper, and cayenne. Dot the salmon with butter and place it in the oven for about 4 minutes. (The salmon will look rare in the middle and more fully cooked on the outside.) Remove from pan. Arrange the fillets on warm plates then sprinkle with herbs. Dust lightly with salt and spice mix and serve.

fresh tuna salad with potatoes and herbs

from ONE POTATO TWO POTATO

serves 4 | This is a looser, uncomposed version of a salade niçoise, with fresh tuna rather than canned. You want whole leaves of herbs for this salad. A mix of basil and parsley alone is nice, but celery leaves add a little bite.

1	pound fresh tuna
	Coarse salt and freshly ground black pepper
12	basil leaves
5	tablespoons olive oil
1	pound red-skinned potatoes, scrubbed
1	tablespoon dry white wine or dry vermouth
1½	cups mixed fresh basil, flat-leaf parsley, and celery leaves
2	teaspoons Dijon mustard
2	tablespoons white wine vinegar
1	red bell pepper, roasted (see Note page 141) and cut into strips
6	anchovy fillets
2	large eggs, hard-cooked (see page 141) and cut into wedges
1	ripe tomato, cut into wedges

Sprinkle the tuna with salt and pepper. Place on a plate, cover with the basil leaves, drizzle with 2 tablespoons of the oil, and leave it to marinate for about 30 minutes, turning it over once or twice.

Put the potatoes in a saucepan, cover with cold water by at least an inch, add a good pinch of salt, and bring to a boil. Reduce the heat to medium, cover partway, and cook until very tender. Drain the potatoes on a rack in the sink.

▼

FOOD & WINE test-kitchen tips

- If you don't have a grill pan as suggested in the recipe, a cast-iron skillet or heavy sauté pan will do fine. Use medium-high heat and cook a standard 1-inch-thick tuna steak for the same time given for a grill pan, about 1½ minutes per side for rare.

- This would make a nice first course too.

  wine recommendation   A wide range of wines will pair well with this dish. Look for a full-bodied white wine, such as white Burgundy, or a low-key red wine, such as Merlot.

While the potatoes are still warm, cut them into chunks, place in a mixing bowl, and drizzle with the wine.

Heat a cast-iron stovetop grill pan over high heat. Brush the basil off the tuna and sear the tuna for 1½ minutes on each side. Cut the tuna into chunks and add to the potatoes, along with the herbs.

Combine the mustard, vinegar, and salt and pepper to taste in a small bowl. Whisk in the remaining 3 tablespoons olive oil.

Add the vinaigrette to the salad, toss well, and pile it on a serving platter. Garnish prettily with the roasted pepper, anchovies, eggs, and tomato.

note Peppers taste great roasted on an open flame, but you can also make them in the oven.

For the flame method, turn on a gas burner and set the pepper in it. Char it all over, turning with tongs, so the skin is black and blistery.

For the oven method, heat the oven to 350 degrees. Place the pepper on a baking sheet or a piece of aluminum foil and cook for about 30 minutes, until the skin has blistered and browned in spots.

Either way you cook the pepper, seal it up in a bag (traditional is brown paper, but plastic does work) for 15 to 20 minutes to steam. Rub off the skin with your fingers or paper towels—never wash it off, never—and tear the pepper open. Pull off the stem and seed pod, trim away the veins, and you're ready to go.

hard-cooked eggs Tender whites, bright yolks still a bit moist in the center—these are hall-marks of a hard-cooked egg that's done properly. Treat an egg wrong, and you end up with rubbery whites and that nasty green ring around the yolk.

You'll read conflicting instructions in just about every cookbook, and you just might have your own ideas, but here's how we've been making them. Cook only as many as you need (we don't much care for hard-boiled eggs if they've been sitting in the refrigerator).

▼

Put the eggs in a saucepan and cover with water. Don't crowd them; they want room. So if you need a lot, use several pans. Bring the water just to a boil over medium to medium-high heat. Once it starts to bubble, turn the heat to the lowest possible setting and set the timer for 8 minutes.

When the timer goes off, turn off the heat and drain off the water. Now give the pan two or three vigorous shakes, which will crack the shells and release any noxious fumes (ever peeled an egg and smelled sulfur?). Cover with cold water, drain, and cover again with cold water. Let the eggs cool completely in the water before you peel them.

lobster and potato salad with tarragon

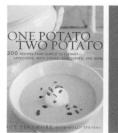

from ONE POTATO TWO POTATO

serves 4 | Here's a happier version of the classic French potato salad known as *salade à la Russe*. The original includes a mix of diced vegetables bound together with a very thick mayonnaise; this one uses fresh tarragon to flavor the mayonnaise and omits the diced carrots, turnips, and pickled tongue of the classic.

Ruby Crescent potatoes give a nice rosy color to the salad, but any small creamer potato will do. For a real summer luncheon salad, line the plates with Bibb lettuce.

> $1\frac{1}{4}$ pounds Ruby Crescent or small creamer potatoes
>
> Coarse salt
>
> $\frac{1}{2}$ pound green beans, topped, tailed, and cut into $1\frac{1}{2}$-inch pieces
> (or substitute fresh sugar snaps, but leave them whole)
>
> 1 red bell pepper, cored, seeded, and diced
>
> $\frac{1}{2}$ pound fresh-cooked lobster meat (picked from about $2\frac{1}{2}$ pounds lobsters)
>
> Freshly ground black pepper
>
> $\frac{1}{4}$ cup heavy cream
>
> $\frac{1}{3}$ cup mayonnaise
>
> $1\frac{1}{2}$ teaspoons chopped fresh tarragon

Put the potatoes in a saucepan, cover with cold water by at least an inch, add a good pinch of salt, and bring to a boil. Reduce the heat to medium, cover partway, and cook until the potatoes are tender. Drain the potatoes on a rack in the sink and let them cool in a single layer.

Bring another pot of salted water to a boil and drop in the beans. Boil until just tender, about 4 minutes. Just before draining the beans, drop the diced red pepper into the water for 20 to 30 seconds. (This takes just the slightest bit of crunch off the pepper dice so they blend better with the other salad ingredients.) Drain the beans and peppers and rinse them immediately with plenty of cold running water. Drain again and then dump onto a clean towel to dry.

▼

FOOD & WINE test-kitchen tips

- To cook two $1\frac{1}{4}$-pound lobsters, drop them into boiling, well-salted water and cook, uncovered, for 10 minutes from the time you put them in the water (even though it's not boiling the whole time).

- Besides being a great luncheon salad, this makes an excellent first course.

wine recommendation American Chardonnay is so powerful that it overwhelms most dishes. However, it finds its match here. Lobster is one of the few things that can stand up to California Chardonnay.

When the potatoes are at room temperature, peel them. It may seem a bit of work to peel these little potatoes, but you're making a fancy French salad. Cut the potatoes into bite-sized pieces and drop them into a bowl.

Chop the lobster meat into bite-sized pieces and add to the potatoes. Add the beans and peppers, season very lightly with salt and pepper, and toss to combine.

Whisk the heavy cream until it is just a bit frothy and beginning to thicken. Whisk in the mayonnaise. Add the tarragon and season with salt and pepper.

You have two options for serving here. You could pour the dressing over the salad and toss to dress, or since the salad is so pretty and colorful as is, you may want to serve it plain and pass the dressing in a sauceboat. We sometimes spoon the salad onto a bed of Bibb lettuce leaves and nap the dressing over the top. Once the salad is dressed, serve it. Undressed, it can be chilled for several hours.

steamed lobster with thai hot sauce

from HOME COOKING AROUND THE WORLD

makes 4 servings | Drawn or clarified butter is the classic "sauce" for dipping and slathering warm pieces of steamed or boiled lobster. But what follows here is a butterless alternative that accents lobster equally well. Taught to me by a friend from Thailand, the sauce is an amazing blend of hot, sour, and salty tastes. In a Thai kitchen, fish sauce would usually be added to provide the saltiness; but in order to enhance and not overpower the delicate flavor of lobster, this recipe substitutes salted water—and what better pairing for something from the sea?

The amount of chiles in this recipe may seem like it's too much—and in fact the sauce is an eyebrow raiser—but the pepper "heat" is balanced by the garlic and lime juice.

thai hot sauce

1/4	cup cold water
1	teaspoon salt
10	cloves garlic, chopped
10	small red hot chiles, stemmed and thinly sliced (for a milder sauce, remove the seeds and membranes)
1/4	cup lime juice (2 to 3 limes), or to taste
4	live lobsters (about 1 1/2 pounds each)

FOOD & WINE test-kitchen tips

- As the recipe states, you want to steam the lobsters, not boil them. Adjust the heat under the steamer so that the water just boils gently. Don't let it boil up so furiously that it engulfs the lobsters.

- After 10 minutes, start testing the lobster every minute or so to see whether you can pull an antenna out easily. As soon as you can, yank the lobster out of the pot to avoid cooking the meat to the chewy stage.

- This terrific Thai Hot Sauce is too good to reserve for one dish. Try it with raw oysters and with hot or cold shrimp as well.

wine recommendation   This dish calls out for an aromatic wine. Look for a bone-dry Riesling from the Rheingau in Germany or Austria's Wachau.

thai hot sauce In a small saucepan, bring the water to a boil. Stir in the salt until dissolved. Remove from heat. In a mortar with a pestle, crush together the garlic and chiles until they form a paste. Stir in the lime juice to taste, working the liquid into the paste. Stir in 3 tablespoons of the salted water and blend well. Taste. If necessary, adjust the balance between hot, sour, and salty. The sauce can also be made in a small food processor or blender. Divide the sauce among 4 small cups and serve as a dipping sauce with the lobster.

lobsters Steaming whole lobsters cooks them more slowly than boiling, thus reducing the chance of overcooking. Figure on about a 5-gallon pot for steaming the lobsters. If the pot is smaller, cook lobsters in two batches. Rig pot with a steamer, or in lieu of that, a metal colander turned upside down. Pour in about an inch or two of sea water, or tap water with about 2 tablespoons salt added. If you can't find anything in your kitchen that will work as a steamer, you can do without. Cover pot and bring water to a boil.

Take the live lobsters, and if the claws are secured with rubber bands, snip bands off with kitchen shears. Be careful. Once one claw is "unleashed," it will move in the direction of your hand as you remove the band from the other claw—but you can move faster than the lobster. Place live lobsters headfirst into steamer rack or directly into boiling water in bottom of pot. Cover and steam for about 14 minutes. When done, the shells will be bright orange-red, tail curled, and antennae easily pulled out.

Using tongs, remove lobsters. Using a clean kitchen towel to protect your hands, break off the knuckles and claws, and cut off the tail. The tail meat should be creamy white, and any roe or eggs should be bright orange-red and solid. Serve with Thai Hot Sauce for dipping.

lobster portuguese-style

from PRIME TIME EMERIL

makes 2 servings | For some, lobster is an extravagance, but where I grew up, they were always available and eaten regularly. We ate them frequently, prepared in all kinds of ways. This Fall River classic reminded me that a little pork sausage can add a world of flavor to just about any dish—even seafood. If you prefer not to split the live lobster in half yourself (it's really no big deal), have the guys at your local fish market do it for you. (Ask them to show you how to do it.) Oh, and make sure you serve this with piles of hot bread for sopping up the broth!

2   cups peeled and diced Idaho potatoes

2   tablespoons olive oil

6   ounces smoked spicy sausage, such as chorizo, removed from casings and chopped

1   cup finely chopped yellow onions

3   tablespoons finely chopped red bell peppers

2   bay leaves

2   tablespoons minced garlic

1   tablespoon minced shallots

2   tablespoons chopped fresh flat-leaf parsley

$^1/_2$ cup chopped pimiento-stuffed green olives

$^1/_2$ cup chopped pitted black olives

$1^1/_2$ cups seeded and chopped tomatoes

1   teaspoon salt, or more to taste

$^1/_2$ teaspoon crushed red pepper flakes, or more to taste

One $1^1/_2$-pound live lobster, split lengthwise in half

$^1/_2$ cup dry white wine

$^1/_4$ cup chopped green onions (green and white parts)

1 Bring the potatoes and enough water to cover to a boil in a small saucepan over high heat. Cook until the potatoes are just tender, about 6 minutes. Drain.

FOOD & WINE test-kitchen tips

- The fastest way to seed tomatoes: cut them all in half horizontally, one by one hold each tomato half cut side down, squeeze gently, and sweep a finger across the surface to get rid of the seeds.

- For $1^1/_2$ cups of chopped tomatoes you'll probably need 3 medium or 2 large, about a pound.

wine recommendation   Portuguese wines can be hard to find but are worth the extra effort. With this lusty dish, try a Vinho Verde made from Alvarinho or Trajadura grapes.

2 Heat the olive oil in a large skillet over medium-high heat. Add the sausage and cook, stirring occasionally, until just beginning to brown, about 5 minutes. Stir in the onions, red bell peppers, and bay leaves and cook until beginning to soften, about 3 minutes. Add the garlic, shallots, and parsley and cook, stirring until fragrant, about 1 minute. Add the olives, potatoes, tomatoes, salt, and crushed red pepper flakes, stir well to combine, and cook for 1 minute.

3 Add the split lobster, shell side down. Add 1 cup water and the wine, cover, and simmer until the lobster shells are deep red and the meat is cooked through, about 10 minutes.

4 With tongs, transfer each lobster half to a shallow soup bowl. Season the broth if necessary, remove the bay leaves, and spoon the broth over the lobster. Garnish with the chopped green onions and serve immediately.

grilled skewers of calamari and shrimp

spiedini di frutti di mare **from BIBA'S TASTE OF ITALY**

serves 4 | This is one of the first dishes I taught when I began my cooking career, because it is simple to prepare and absolutely delicious. This preparation, from Quattro Colonne Trattoria in Rimini, briefly marinates shellfish in flavorful olive oil with bread crumbs, parsley, and garlic before grilling. When the bread begins to char a bit, forming a golden, crisp coating, the cooking is done.

Follow these delicious *spiedini* with a salad of ripe tomatoes, basil, and olive oil.

$3/4$ pound cleaned squid

$1 1/2$ pounds medium shrimp, peeled and deveined

1   garlic clove, very finely chopped

$1/3$ cup extra virgin olive oil

$1/4$ cup chopped flat-leaf parsley

$1/3$ cup fine dried bread crumbs

Salt and freshly ground black pepper to taste

Lemon wedges

Cut the squid bodies into $1 1/2$-inch-wide rings. Reserve the tentacles for another use. Wash the shrimp under cold running water and pat dry with paper towels.

In a medium bowl, mix the garlic with the oil, parsley, and bread crumbs. Season with salt and pepper. Add the squid and shrimp and toss to coat well. Cover the bowl and marinate at room temperature for 30 to 40 minutes.

FOOD & WINE test-kitchen tips

- Squid and calamari are the same thing. Small ones are preferable here. The really big, thick ones will usually be tough when grilled, even for a short time.

- The portions in this recipe are generous. If you don't like calamari or can't find small ones, leave them out. You'll have plenty with just the shrimp.

- We found that $1 1/2$ teaspoons salt and $3/4$ teaspoon pepper were a good amount of seasoning for the bread crumb mixture.

- You'll need 4 long metal or wooden skewers—or a bunch of short ones.

wine recommendation   Bianco di Custoza from southern Italy will make an excellent match without breaking the bank. If you're celebrating a special occasion, look for an aged white Bordeaux.

Preheat a grill or the broiler. Thread the squid onto 4 metal or wooden skewers, pressing the bread crumb mixture back onto the squid if necessary. Thread the shrimp onto separate skewers, pressing the coating onto the shrimp if necessary. (Because the squid cooks faster than the shrimp, the two need to be skewered separately.)

Place the shrimp skewers on the hot grill or on a baking sheet under the broiler and cook until a golden crust forms on one side, about 2 minutes. Turn them over and cook until the other side is golden and crisp, 1 to 2 minutes longer. When you turn the shrimp, place the squid skewers next to them. As soon as one side turns golden, about 1 minute, turn them over to brown the other side. (Do not cook the squid for more than 1 to 2 minutes total, or they will become tough and rubbery.) Serve at once, with lemon wedges.

clams steamed in sake

from **A NEW WAY TO COOK** | serves 2

I often make this dish when I want an utterly quick and delicious meal. Sake, the Japanese rice wine, enriched with a little butter makes a sweeter, mellower sauce than white wine makes. It goes very well over egg pasta.

1½ cups sake

2   pounds small clams, such as littlenecks or Manila, scrubbed, or mussels, scrubbed and debearded (if necessary)

1   tablespoon cold unsalted butter

1   teaspoon minced shallots

Pinch of kosher salt

2   tablespoons chopped fresh cilantro, basil, or flat-leaf parsley

In a medium nonreactive saucepan, simmer the sake over moderate heat until reduced by half, 8 to 10 minutes. Add the clams, cover, and cook until they have opened, 3 to 4 minutes. Using a slotted spoon, transfer the clams to two warm shallow soup bowls.

Swirl the butter, shallots, and salt into the sake broth, bring to a boil over high heat, and boil for 30 seconds. Ladle the sauce over the clams and garnish with the herbs. Serve at once.

how to debeard mussels   The "beard" of a mussel is a fibrous tuft that the mussel uses to anchor itself to rocks. To remove it, grasp it tightly, as close to the shell as possible, with your thumb and forefinger and pull it off.

FOOD & WINE test-kitchen tips

- Clams can be quite saline. It's a good idea to taste the broth before adding any salt.

- These clams would make a nice first course too, in which case the recipe would serve four.

wine recommendation   To match the lightness of this dish, try one of the featherweights of the wine world, a dry Muscat from Alsace or Austria.

new england clam and sweet potato chowder

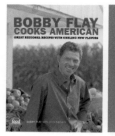

from BOBBY FLAY COOKS AMERICAN

serves 8 | You chowder purists will just have to trust me on this one. As a big fan of sweet potatoes, I like to substitute them for white ones in traditional recipes. They make for a great chowder, with a hint of color and a note of sweetness that sets this recipe apart. Smoky bacon pulls all the great flavors—clams, potatoes, and cream—together and cuts through the richness. With a salad and bread, this makes a comforting one-dish meal. Or just serve with crisp oyster crackers.

2 cups white wine

2 cups water

48 littleneck clams, scrubbed

Bottled clam juice (optional)

2 cups heavy cream

2 cups whole milk

$1/4$ pound slab bacon, cut into $1/4$-inch dice

2 medium onions, chopped

2 stalks celery, cut into $1/4$-inch dice

2 tablespoons flour

2 large sweet potatoes, peeled and cut into $1/2$-inch dice

Salt and freshly ground white pepper

Hot sauce

1 Bring the wine and water to a boil in a large covered saucepan. Add the clams, cover the pot, and cook, shaking the pan occasionally, until all of the clams have opened. Discard any clams that have not opened. Lift out the clams with a slotted spoon and set aside. Strain the liquid through a fine strainer into a bowl. This should yield about 5 cups liquid; add bottled clam juice to make 6 cups. Remove the clams from their shells and roughly chop the meat.

▼

FOOD & WINE test-kitchen tips

- The amount of seasoning needed in this chowder will depend entirely on your clams. Some are saltier than others, so taste carefully. We added $2^{1}/_{2}$ teaspoons salt. And though white pepper is called for, probably to avoid specks in a creamy white dish, we liked black just fine.

- Chowder always makes a luscious first course as well.

wine recommendation An unoaked Chardonnay from South Africa or New Zealand will have just enough heft to take on the full flavors of this robust soup.

2   Combine the heavy cream and milk in a medium saucepan and bring to a boil. Reduce heat to low and simmer until reduced by half.

3   Meanwhile, cook the bacon in a large saucepan over medium-high heat, stirring often, until golden brown. Transfer the bacon to a plate and pour off all but 3 tablespoons of the bacon fat. Add the onions and celery to the pan and cook until soft. Add the flour and cook, stirring constantly, for 2 minutes. Add the reserved clam broth, stir well, and bring to a simmer. Add the potatoes and cook until just soft but not mushy.

4   Add the cream mixture to the chowder and heat through over low heat. Add the chopped clams and the bacon, mix well, and season with salt, white pepper, and hot sauce to taste.

fish & shellfish

chicken & other main dishes

pecan-crusted chicken

from PRIME TIME EMERIL | makes 4 servings

With its crunchy nut coating, this oven-baked chicken comes close to fried. Boy, the pecan flavor is delicious! This is a great dish to make when you have a hankering for fried chicken, but don't have the time to spend in front of the stove. Make it ahead and take it along with you on a picnic or to a tailgate party, like we did on a food-to-go show.

1   cup buttermilk

3   tablespoons Emeril's Original Essence or
     Creole Seasoning (page 93)

2   teaspoons salt

One 3$^{1}/_{2}$-pound chicken, cut into 8 pieces
     (or 8 chicken parts of your choosing)

2   tablespoons olive oil

$^{3}/_{4}$ cup pecan pieces

$^{3}/_{4}$ cup bleached all-purpose flour

$^{1}/_{2}$ teaspoon freshly ground black pepper

1   Combine the buttermilk, 1 tablespoon of the Essence, and 1 teaspoon of the salt in a large (1-gallon) plastic storage bag. Add the chicken pieces, seal, and gently squeeze to coat the chicken evenly. Refrigerate for at least 1 hour, or up to 4 hours.

2   Preheat the oven to 400°F. Grease a heavy baking sheet with the olive oil and set aside.

3   Pulse the pecans in a food processor or blender until finely chopped into a meal.

4   Combine the ground pecans, the flour, the remaining 2 tablespoons Essence and 1 teaspoon salt, and the pepper in another large plastic bag.

FOOD & WINE test-kitchen tips

- If you use another brand of bottled Creole seasoning mix instead of Emeril's, halve the salt in the pecan coating. Some mixes that are on the market have more salt than anything else.

- To ensure crispness on all sides when you're serving this at room temperature, transfer the chicken to a rack to cool rather than leaving it on the baking sheet.

wine recommendation
Gutsy seasoning calls for a gutsy wine. Seek out a full-bodied, slightly spicy Viognier. The varietal was born in the Rhône Valley but is equally at home in California and the South of France.

5 Remove the chicken from the buttermilk mixture. Add the chicken one piece at a time to the pecan-flour mixture, and shake to coat evenly. Put the chicken skin side down on the prepared baking sheet.

6 Bake the chicken for 30 minutes, then turn it. Return to the oven and bake until the juices run clear when pierced with a fork, about 30 minutes. Serve hot, or let cool to room temperature.

pan-roasted chicken with cognac-peppercorn sauce

from SECOND HELPINGS FROM UNION SQUARE CAFE

serves 4 | The cooking method for this wonderful dish is a good example of a true French sauté. Here, the chicken and aromatic elements are cooked through before the sauce is prepared at the end. The presentation is rustic, with all the herbs and spices left in the sauce. Accompany the chicken with broccoli and fried potatoes.

1   (4 to 4$\frac{1}{2}$-pound) chicken, cut into 10 pieces
    (drumsticks, thighs, wings, and split breast)

1$\frac{1}{2}$ teaspoons kosher salt

$\frac{1}{4}$ teaspoon freshly ground black pepper

2   tablespoons vegetable oil

$\frac{1}{3}$ cup thinly sliced garlic

4   sprigs fresh thyme, coarsely chopped

6   bay leaves

20   whole peppercorns

$\frac{1}{4}$ cup Cognac

$\frac{1}{4}$ cup white wine

1   cup brown Chicken Stock (next page) or
    store-bought veal stock (or demi-glace)

1   tablespoon Dijon mustard

1$\frac{1}{2}$ tablespoons butter

1   Heat the oven to 375 degrees F.

2   Place the chicken pieces in a large bowl. Sprinkle with 1 teaspoon of salt and $\frac{1}{4}$ teaspoon of pepper and toss to season.

FOOD & WINE test-kitchen tips

- You'll need to cut each half breast in two crosswise to get 10 nice pieces of chicken.

- To avoid having the chicken skin stick to your pan, don't move the pieces for the first 5 minutes of browning.

160

3 Place an 11-inch skillet over high heat, add the oil, and heat until smoking. Add the chicken pieces and brown them on all sides, about 10 minutes. Turn the chicken so the pieces are skin side down, transfer to the oven, and bake until the breast meat is cooked through, 10 to 15 minutes. Remove the pan from the oven, transfer the breast pieces to a serving platter, and cover to keep warm. Add the garlic, thyme, bay leaves, and peppercorns to the skillet, sprinkling them around the remaining pieces of chicken. Return the skillet to the oven and continue baking until the chicken is cooked through, an additional 5 to 10 minutes.

4 Transfer the remaining pieces of chicken to the serving platter and cover. Place the skillet over medium-high heat and cook 1 to 2 minutes to lightly brown the garlic. Pour the fat from the skillet, being careful to leave in the herbs and spices.

5 Away from the open flame, pour the Cognac into the skillet. Return to the heat and reduce until almost dry. Pour in the wine and reduce until almost dry. Add the stock and any juices from the serving platter, bring to a simmer, and reduce until somewhat thickened. Whisk in the mustard and butter and season with 1/2 teaspoon of salt. Return the chicken to the skillet and warm over low heat. Transfer the chicken, covered with sauce, herbs, and spices, to a warm platter and serve.

wine suggestions The assertive flavors would make the chicken work quite well with a spicy and juicy syrah from California, Australia, or the Rhône Valley.

chicken stock | **makes 3 quarts** | A clear, flavorful chicken stock is indispensable for sauces, soups, and most risotto recipes. The key to a clear, brilliant stock is to skim as much fat and foam as possible from the surface, and to cook the stock at a barely perceptible simmer. For a brown chicken stock, a darker, more richly flavored stock that can be substituted for veal stock, roast the chicken bones with the vegetables and 1 tablespoon of tomato paste in a 350-degree oven for 30 minutes, or until browned. Add the water, herbs, and spices and proceed with the recipe that follows. In addition to getting chicken bones from your butcher, use leftover carcasses from roast chicken.

▼

5	pounds chicken bones, rinsed well in cold water
4	quarts water
1	large onion, coarsely chopped (2$\frac{1}{2}$ cups)
3	medium carrots, scrubbed and quartered (2$\frac{1}{2}$ cups)
3	celery ribs, quartered
1	medium parsnip, peeled and coarsely chopped (1$\frac{1}{2}$ cups)
1	bay leaf
1	teaspoon fresh thyme
10	whole black peppercorns
$\frac{1}{4}$	cup fresh parsley sprigs

1 Combine all the ingredients in an 8-quart stockpot. Over medium heat, bring slowly to a boil. Skim the foam that rises to the surface with a ladle.

2 Reduce the heat and simmer very slowly, uncovered, for 4 to 5 hours. Skim the surface with a ladle every 30 minutes to remove any accumulated fat or impurities.

3 Strain the stock into a clean pot or metal bowl and set it over a large bowl filled with ice. Refrigerate for 1 or 2 days, or freeze for several months. Remove any hardened fat from refrigerated stock before reheating.

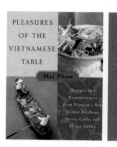

grilled five-spice chicken *ga ngu vi huong*

from PLEASURES OF THE VIETNAMESE TABLE

serves 4 | The best five-spice chicken I have had in Vietnam was made by a street food vendor in the port town of Hoi An in the central region. The vendor used a spice mix of freshly toasted star anise and turmeric. When she grilled the chicken, the whole neighborhood was perfumed with the most enticing fragrance. This is my version of that dish. It's great with Vietnamese fried rice and Cucumber Salad (page 186).

1	whole chicken (about 2¹/₂ pounds), preferably free range, rinsed
3	tablespoons vegetable oil
2	tablespoons soy sauce
3	tablespoons minced ginger
2	tablespoons minced garlic
2	tablespoons sugar
2	teaspoons ground turmeric
1	teaspoon Chinese five-spice powder (page 164)
¹/₂	tablespoon sea salt
4	whole star anise, lightly toasted in a dry pan for 3 minutes, pounded or ground into a fine powder
¹/₂	cup Soy-Lime Dipping Sauce (page 165)

1 Cut the chicken into 6 pieces and make 1 or 2 slashes in each piece for faster cooking. Trim and discard any excess fat. Pat the chicken dry.

2 In a bowl, combine the oil, soy sauce, ginger, garlic, sugar, turmeric, five-spice powder and salt. Stir well to blend. Add the chicken pieces and turn several times to coat them evenly. Marinate in the refrigerator for at least 4 hours.

▼

FOOD & WINE test-kitchen tips

- If you're pressed for time, don't hesitate to omit the Soy-Lime Dipping Sauce. The chicken is plenty tasty without it.

- Another time-saver is to buy a chicken that's already cut up. Or you can just get 2¹/₂ pounds of the pieces you like best.

wine recommendation A wine made from the aromatic Gewurztraminer grape will mirror the spiciness of this dish. For elegance, try a wine from the Alsace region of France. If you prefer a more assertive style, seek out a bottle from California or Australia.

3 Start a charcoal grill or preheat a gas grill to moderate heat. (You can also use a broiler.) Thirty minutes before cooking, add the freshly toasted star anise powder to the marinated chicken, turning so the meat is coated evenly.

4 Place the chicken, skin side up, on the grill. Cook 10 minutes, then turn over and grill until the chicken is cooked and the juices run clear, another 10 minutes, depending on the thickness. While grilling, move the chicken pieces around so that they cook evenly. Transfer the chicken to a serving platter and serve with the dipping sauce.

five-spice powder *ngu vi huong* Five-spice powder is a traditional Chinese spice blend that can be made with more than five spices. This fragrant brown powder is principally made with star anise and cinnamon and several other ingredients such as Szechuan peppercorns, clove, and fennel. It's often used to season roasted and braised meats, especially chicken and duck.

soy-lime dipping sauce nuoc tuong pha | **makes about 1 cup** | This vegetarian dipping sauce can be made with any soy sauce, including the Japanese-style Kikkoman, although the Vietnamese prefer the lighter-bodied Chinese-style products marketed under the brands Kim Lan, Bo De and Pearl River Bridge. Like dipping sauces made with fish sauce, you can embellish this with different aromatics such as ginger and cilantro.

1   clove garlic

2   fresh Thai bird chilies

$2^1/_2$ tablespoons sugar

$^1/_3$ cup soy sauce, preferably Chinese style

$2^1/_2$ tablespoons fresh lime juice with pulp

$^1/_4$ cup water, or to taste

1   Place the garlic, chilies and sugar in a mortar and pound into a paste. (You can also chop the garlic and chilies by hand.) Transfer to a small bowl and add the soy sauce, lime juice and water. Stir until well blended. This sauce will keep up to 3 weeks if stored in the refrigerator in a tight-lidded jar.

FOOD & WINE test-kitchen tips

- If you can't get Thai bird chilies, use whatever hot chilies are available. We used jalapeños.

- Leftover Soy-Lime Dipping Sauce is no problem. It's good with any plain roasted or grilled chicken, with pork, and with steamed or stir-fried vegetables.

roast chicken with fennel and sage from NAPA STORIES

serves 4 | I wanted to do a main course for the Mondavi Christmas party that would have meaning for Bob Mondavi. We talked about it and discovered that we both remembered harvesting wild fennel as kids. (In fact, in adulthood, I found a stand of wild fennel at the Robert Mondavi Winery that I used to raid on occasion.)

This roast chicken is seasoned generously with fennel seed, although by all means use wild fennel fronds and seeds if you have them. The halved carrots support the chicken as it cooks and eliminate the need for a rack. While the chicken cooks, prepare the potatoes and fennel for the oven so they can go in as soon as the chicken comes out. If you have two ovens, you can cook the vegetables at the same time.

1	tablespoon sea salt, preferably gray salt (see Note page 169)
1	tablespoon toasted fennel seed
2	tablespoons finely minced fresh sage
	Extra virgin olive oil
	One 3-pound free-range chicken
2	carrots, halved lengthwise

Preheat oven to 450° F. Turn on the convection fan, if you have one.

Pound salt, fennel, and sage together in a mortar, or crush in a mini-chopper or with the flat side of a chef's knife. Coat your hands with olive oil and massage the bird all over. Rub the spice mixture all over the chicken, pressing it into the skin and sprinkling some inside the cavity. Truss the legs.

Line a baking sheet with aluminum foil and oil the foil lightly. Place carrots in the middle of the baking sheet, cut side down and parallel, to make a raft for the bird. Set the chicken on top of the carrots. Bake until chicken begins to color nicely, about 25 minutes, then reduce oven temperature to 375° F and continue roasting until chicken juices run clear, about 35 minutes more. Set chicken aside to rest but leave oven on. While it rests, bake the potatoes and fennel.

▼

FOOD & WINE test-kitchen tips

- The resting time in this recipe is not just a matter of convenience. Your chicken will be much juicier if you don't cut into it right away. If you put the fennel in the oven before the chicken is done, you should still allow at least 10 minutes for the bird to rest.

wine recommendation Choose either a white or a red wine for this flexible dish. If you're in the mood for white, try a Mâcon-Villages; if red, a Sancerre.

roast creamer potatoes | **serves 4**

1 1/2 pounds small boiling potatoes ("creamers"),
about 1 inch in diameter, halved

3 tablespoons extra virgin olive oil

3 tablespoons drippings from roast chicken

20 whole fresh sage leaves

8 whole garlic cloves, unpeeled, stem end trimmed

Sea salt, preferably gray salt (see Note next page)

Cover potatoes with salted water and bring to a boil. Simmer uncovered until they are three-quarters done, 5 to 8 minutes, then drain.

Heat olive oil in a large ovenproof skillet over moderately high heat. When oil is hot, add the potatoes and the drippings. Turn potatoes cut side down. Let them form a good crust, tossing occasionally, then add sage leaves, garlic, and salt and toss for a minute or two. Transfer to the 375° F oven and bake until potatoes are tender when pierced, about 15 minutes.

FOOD & WINE test-kitchen tips

- If you can't find small potatoes, use big ones cut into approximately 1-by-1-inch squares, 1/2 inch thick.

- You may well want to make these potatoes even when you're not roasting a chicken. Lacking chicken drippings, you can use those from whatever bird or beast you're roasting. Or substitute butter. Or just double the olive oil.

bob's braised fennel | serves 4

    2   large bulbs fennel,
         sliced lengthwise ¼-inch thick
    Butter for the baking dish
    Sea salt, preferably gray salt (see Note below)
    Freshly ground black pepper
    Chicken broth

Arrange sliced fennel in one layer in a flameproof buttered baking dish. (You may need two dishes.) Season with salt and pepper. Add enough broth to come halfway up the sides of the fennel. Bring to a boil on top of the stove, then cover and place in the 375° F oven. Bake until fennel is tender, about 30 minutes.

note Gray salt from France's Brittany coast is my favorite salt for most uses. It is moist and chunky and full of flavor from minerals found in the ocean. To make it easier to use for everyday seasoning, I dry large quantities of it in a 200° F oven for 1 hour, then pound it or grind it in a spice grinder until medium-coarse.

FOOD & WINE test-kitchen tips

- If you don't have a flameproof baking dish with a lid, choose any pan that can be used on top of the stove as well as in the oven, and cover it with aluminum foil.

- Want to try the gray salt mentioned here? You may find it labeled simply "sea salt"; if it's gray and in relatively large, irregular crystals, you've got the right stuff.

chicken & other main dishes

roast goose

from SECOND HELPINGS FROM UNION SQUARE CAFE

serves 5 to 6 | When R. W. Apple requested this recipe for a feature article he was writing for the *New York Times* just before Christmas 2000, we had no idea how much enthusiasm it would arouse among food-loving friends everywhere. There wasn't nearly enough stove space at the restaurant to keep up with the demand generated by the article, and we received literally hundreds of requests for reprints of the recipe. Roasting a goose at home is a labor of love: it can be cumbersome and takes some patience. But it's technically a cinch to pull off, and you and your guests will be absolutely delighted with the tender, succulent results. Our trick is to roast the bird "slow and low"—allowing it to self-baste as the layer of fat between the skin and meat renders, and the skin becomes golden and crisp. By all means, save as much of the rendered goose fat as you have room to store. It's the tastiest medium you'll ever use for frying fabulous potatoes (stir in some minced garlic and parsley at the last minute), and is indispensable for making any type of confit. With the goose, we serve baked sauerkraut and apple and mortadella stuffing. Another good option is horseradish-mashed potatoes.

1	10-pound goose
1	small onion, peeled and coarsely chopped
1	stalk celery, coarsely chopped
1	small carrot, washed and coarsely chopped
1	small apple or quince, cored and coarsely chopped
1	bay leaf
8–10	sage leaves, coarsely chopped
$1/2$	teaspoon caraway seeds
10	juniper berries, lightly crushed
	Freshly ground black pepper
2	teaspoons kosher salt
1	cup apple cider
2	cups chicken broth

FOOD & WINE *test-kitchen tips*

- For those who are not keen on even slightly sweet sauces: use 3 cups of chicken broth rather than 2 and omit the cup of apple cider, or simply leave out the cider and boil the mixture for a shorter time so that it reduces less, to $1^1/2$ cups.

- In addition to the uses for leftover goose fat mentioned in the recipe, we suggest: almost anywhere you want a wonderful-tasting fat. Try it in biscuits, pizza dough, or piecrust; use it to sauté vegetables or chicken; give it a whirl in fried rice; dress cabbage, sauerkraut, kale, or other greens with it; substitute it for lard in Mexican dishes such as carnitas or refried beans.

1   Cut away the two end joints of each goose wing and set them aside along with the liver and giblets.

2   Combine the onion, celery, carrot, apple, bay leaf, sage, caraway, juniper, some black pepper, and 1½ teaspoons salt in a small bowl. Stuff the cavity of the goose with the seasoned vegetable mixture. Tie the legs together with a piece of kitchen twine. The goose can be prepared to this stage the day before and held, uncovered, in the refrigerator.

3   Preheat the oven to 250 degrees F. Place the stuffed goose breast-side down on a roasting rack in a large, heavy-bottomed roasting pan, cover the pan tightly with aluminum foil, and place in the oven. Allow the goose to cook for 4 hours.

4   Remove the roasting pan from the oven and uncover the goose, reserving the foil. Turn the oven to 350 degrees F. Lift the rack with the goose from the roasting pan, carefully pour off the fat from the pan, strain it, and reserve, refrigerated or frozen. (The fat will keep for a month or so, well covered in the refrigerator, and indefinitely in the freezer. Use it to make goose or duck confit, to fry potato slices, or to sear meat.) Replace the goose, still breast-side down on the rack, in the roasting pan, return the pan to the oven, and cook, uncovered, for 1 hour.

5   Remove the pan from the oven and scatter the wings, liver, and giblets around the goose. Turn the goose breast-side up, and continue cooking for an additional hour, or until the skin is crisp and golden brown and the leg begins to come away from the body of the goose when gently tugged.

6   Remove the goose to a platter and cover lightly with the foil. Remove the rack from the pan and pour off any fat, leaving the wings, liver, and giblets in the pan. Uncover the goose, cut the twine holding the legs together, and scoop the vegetables from inside the goose and into the roasting pan. Re-cover the goose on the platter, and place the roasting pan on medium heat over one or two burners on the stove. Cook the vegetables, stirring occasionally, for two minutes. Pour in the apple cider and chicken broth and boil liquid until reduced by half. Season with the remaining salt and some additional black pepper, and strain the sauce.

7   Carve the goose and serve with the sauce.

wine suggestions   For white, go with a top-quality Alsatian riesling or Tokay pinot gris. If you're in the mood for red, use a reasonably tannic zinfandel, cabernet sauvignon, or Bordeaux.

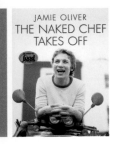

JAMIE OLIVER
THE NAKED CHEF
TAKES OFF

farfalle with savoy cabbage, pancetta, thyme and mozzarella

from THE NAKED CHEF TAKES OFF | serves 4

10	strips of pancetta or lean bacon, thinly sliced
	Olive oil
1	clove of garlic, finely chopped
1	good handful of thyme, leaves picked from stems
1	large Savoy cabbage (outer leaves removed), quartered, cored and finely sliced
1	handful of grated Parmesan cheese
1	lb dried farfalle, the best you can get
	Salt and freshly ground black pepper
	Extra-virgin olive oil
7	oz buffalo mozzarella, cut into $1/2$-inch dice
2	handfuls of pine nuts, lightly toasted

In a pan fry your pancetta in a little olive oil until lightly golden. Add the garlic and thyme and cook until softened. Add the Savoy cabbage and Parmesan, then stir and put the lid on the pan. Cook for a further 5 minutes, shaking every now and again, while you cook your farfalle in salted boiling water until al dente. When the cabbage is nice and tender, season and loosen with some nice peppery extra-virgin olive oil. Toss the drained farfalle into the cabbage mixture and at the last minute mix in the mozzarella and pine nuts. Serve immediately.

FOOD & WINE test-kitchen tips

- Buffalo mozzarella can be hard to find. Any fresh mozzarella you can get should be fine for this recipe.
- You can substitute parsley for the fresh thyme here.

wine recommendation Though hard to find, Swiss Dôle (a blend of Pinot Noir and Gamay) or a Swiss Pinot Noir would be perfect with this dish. A young California Pinot Noir will also work well.

mozzarella in carrozza
mozzarella in a buggy from SOFFRITTO

serves 6 | *Mozzarella in carrozza* is a typical Neapolitan dish. Since it is so difficult, I have included it here because once you have mastered it you will be ready to fry anything. Because of the difficulty of frying something that melts when exposed to heat, there is a remarkable wealth of methods aimed at solving such a problem. After trial and error, I believe the one detailed here to be the most suitable. The salted anchovies and sage are not included in the original recipe, but are additions I heartily suggest. A radicchio salad is a good accompaniment to this main dish.

8	ounces (250 g) fresh buffalo mozzarella, drained (see next page)
2	ounces (50 g) salted anchovies
12	(1/2-inch- or 1-cm-thick) slices dry bread
6	leaves sage, chopped
1	tablespoon all-purpose (plain) flour
2	eggs
Salt	
1/3	cup (75 ml) milk
Extra virgin olive oil, for frying	

Place the mozzarella in a dish, cover, and leave to drain overnight in the refrigerator so that it loses as much water as possible.

Cut the drained mozzarella into 1/2-inch (1-cm) slices. Rinse the anchovies thoroughly under a trickle of water. With your hands, open the back of each anchovy, remove the backbone, and divide into 2 fillets. Cut each of the fillets into 3 pieces. Now make "sandwiches" like this: a slice of bread, a slice of mozzarella, an anchovy fillet cut in 3 pieces, a chopped sage leaf, and a slice of bread. Holding together these sandwiches as well as possible, dredge their edges in the flour. Then beat the eggs thoroughly with a pinch of salt and the milk, trying to make this rather fluid batter as smooth as possible. Dip the "sandwiches" in the batter, first on one side and then on the other. The bread will soak up the liquid and become very floppy, hence the difficulty of frying it.

Put just enough oil in the skillet to submerge the lower bread slice and not quite reach the mozzarella (a little less than ½ inch or 1 cm). Heat the oil over medium-high heat until little bubbles begin to form. Check the temperature of the oil by tossing in some bread crumbs; it will be ready when they sizzle. Using a flat, slotted spatula, carry each *mozzarella in carrozza* to the frying pan without breaking it. Slip them into the oil, no more than 2 at a time, and turn down the heat a bit, if necessary, to gently fry the sandwiches. Fry until they are crispy and golden, about 2 minutes on each side. Turn them once, lifting them up with the spatula and using a second spatula on top: Gently squeeze to hold the sandwich together, and let it slide into the oil to fry the other side. Remove the sandwiches from the oil and place on absorbent paper to drain while you fry the others. Serve immediately.

mozzarella cheese There are two kinds of true mozzarella, a soft, wet cheese that is kept moist in its own whey until it is used. The most famous, called *di bufala*, is made in the region of Naples with part or all buffalo milk. The other, *fiordilatte*, is made entirely from cow's milk. Mozzarella comes in various sizes, from the bite-size *bocconcino* to pieces weighing more than four pounds. It must be used very fresh, no more than two or three days from the time it is made. Buffalo mozzarella is also smoked using wheat straw. A few Neapolitan dairies in North America make mozzarella. Avoid the mass-produced stuff that is sold in plastic packages in supermarkets; it tastes more of plastic than of cheese.

FOOD & WINE test-kitchen tips

- You'll want bread that is just a little bigger in diameter than the mozzarella.

- The recipe calls for dry bread. If all you have is fresh, just slice it ahead of time and put it on a rack to dry a bit.

wine recommendation In order to balance the intense flavors of the anchovy fillets, an uncomplicated wine high in acidity is needed. Muscadet, from France's Loire Valley, will do the trick.

ten-minute roasted leek and gruyère soufflé

from JOANNE WEIR'S MORE COOKING IN THE WINE COUNTRY

serves 8 | Get your guests to the table and then serve them this ingenious soufflé that bakes in ten minutes rather than the customary sixty! We used to make a soufflé like this at Chez Panisse and it really is amazing, especially when it's baked in a beautiful oval oven-proof platter, such as one of the French porcelain platters that are widely available in this country. It makes a great main course with a salad—or it can be a first course.

2	tablespoons extra virgin olive oil
4	leeks, white and 2 inches green part, cut into ¼-inch dice
1	teaspoon chopped fresh thyme

Salt and freshly ground black pepper

2½ cups half-and-half

5	tablespoons unsalted butter
5	tablespoons all-purpose flour
6	eggs, separated, room temperature
1	cup (4 ounces) grated Gruyère cheese
1	cup finely grated Parmigiano-Reggiano cheese

Warm the olive oil in a large skillet over medium-high heat. Add the leeks, thyme, and salt and pepper to taste. Reduce the heat to low and cook, stirring occasionally, until the leeks are soft and just starting to turn lightly golden, 40 to 45 minutes. Remove from the heat and let cool.

Pour the half-and-half into a saucepan and bring it almost to the boiling point.

▼

FOOD & WINE test-kitchen tips

- Leeks need a good washing since they tend to harbor dirt between their layers. Put them in a colander and rinse under running water *after* they're diced.

- For this recipe, you'll need about a teaspoon of salt altogether.

- The center of the cooked soufflé is much softer than the edges. The contrast is lovely, so make sure everybody gets some of each.

Meanwhile, melt the butter in a heavy saucepan over medium heat. Add the flour and whisk 1 to 2 minutes. Add the scalded half-and-half to the flour mixture, stirring rapidly with a whisk. Cook for 3 to 4 minutes, until the sauce is smooth and thick. Add salt and pepper to taste.

Add the egg yolks to the cream sauce, one at a time, stirring well after each addition. Add the Gruyère, 1/2 cup of the Parmigiano, and salt and pepper to taste. Add the cooled leeks to the cream sauce. Mix well.

Preheat the oven to 450°F.

While the oven is heating, place the egg whites in a clean bowl and beat until they form stiff peaks. Fold half of the whites into the cheese mixture with as few strokes as possible. Then fold in the remaining whites. Pour the mixture onto a generously buttered 18-inch oval ovenproof dish (or two 12-inch ovals). Sprinkle the top with the remaining 1/2 cup Parmigiano. Bake on the top shelf of the oven until puffed and well browned, 10 to 14 minutes.

wine suggestion Pinot Noir or Cabernet Sauvignon

leek and potato tart

from ONE POTATO TWO POTATO

makes one 15-inch tart | We make a meal of this free-form tart with just a salad on the side and sliced oranges for dessert. If you want, you can transform this into a vegetarian dish by cutting out the bacon; add water by the tablespoon if the leeks start to dry out when you're wilting them.

for the pastry

$1^{1}/_{2}$ cups all-purpose flour

Coarse salt

12 tablespoons ($1^{1}/_{2}$ sticks) cold unsalted butter, cut into bits

1 large egg yolk

for the filling

2 tablespoons unsalted butter

2 or 3 slices bacon, chopped

$3^{1}/_{2}$ cups sliced leeks (white and light green parts of 3–4 leeks)

Coarse salt and freshly ground black pepper

$^{3}/_{4}$ pound cold boiled all-purpose potatoes,
     peeled and cut into $^{1}/_{2}$-inch chunks

1 cup heavy cream

Freshly grated nutmeg

2 ounces Emmentaler or Gruyère cheese, shredded (about $^{1}/_{2}$ cup)

for the pastry Put the flour in a bowl and add a good pinch of salt. Stir with a fork. Add the butter, toss it in the flour, and then cut it into the flour with a pastry cutter or your fingers. You want something that looks like very coarse oatmeal, with some larger bits of butter. Drop in the yolk and work with your fingers to distribute it evenly. Add 1 tablespoon ice water, toss the pastry with a fork, and continue adding ice water and tossing and stirring with the fork until the pastry comes together. You may need as much as 4 tablespoons water. Gather the pastry into a ball, then form it into a disk on a lightly floured countertop. Wrap it in plastic and refrigerate for 30 minutes.

Heat the oven to 350 degrees.

▼

for the filling Heat the butter in a large skillet over medium heat. Add the bacon and cook until the fat has rendered and the bacon is beginning to brown. Raise the heat to medium-high, add the leeks, season with salt and pepper, and cook until the leeks are wilted and tender, about 7 minutes. Add the potatoes and cook for 3 to 5 minutes, until the potatoes just begin to brown.

Pour in ¼ cup of the cream and cook, stirring and scraping the bottom of the pan, until the cream is mostly absorbed. Continue adding cream by ¼-cup increments until it's all been mostly absorbed and the mixture is thick but still juicy. Remove it from the heat, grate in some nutmeg, and taste for salt and pepper.

Roll the pastry out to a 17-inch circle on a lightly floured counter. Transfer it to a parchment-lined baking sheet. Spread it with the leek mixture, leaving a border of about 2½ inches all around. Strew the cheese over the top, and fold the border back over the filling.

Bake the tart for about 40 minutes, until it's bubbling and well browned. You can serve this hot or at room temperature.

cleaning leeks Here's a fast way to prepare leeks, to make sure they're free of sand: Trim off the roots and the tough green parts (we use the tender green parts except in vichyssoise, where a pale color is important). Halve the leeks lengthwise and cut into thin half-moons. Put the leeks in a big bowl and cover with cold water. Swirl them around a few times, then leave them for a few minutes. Lift the leeks out into a colander—don't pour: you'll just redistribute the dirt. If there's a lot of grit left in the bowl, rinse it out and repeat the process, but one quick bath is usually enough.

FOOD & WINE test-kitchen tips

- Since there's not much salt in the pastry, we found that we needed about 1 teaspoon salt in the filling.

- Home ovens almost never hit the desired temperature on the nose, let alone maintain a consistent heat. Bake this admirable tart following the words in the recipe "until it's bubbling and well browned" rather than sticking slavishly to the time estimate given. We needed to cook it for about 50 minutes.

- The tart also makes a luscious first course. Or you can cut it into tiny wedges for an hors d'oeuvre.

wine recommendation White wine from the Rhône Valley can be hard to find but is well worth the search. The smoothness of the wine will marry effectively with the creamy flavor of the tart.

chicken & other main dishes

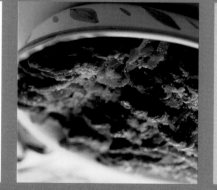

vegetables
& other side
dishes

mushrooms in a scallion dressing *kinoko no aemono* japan

from MADHUR JAFFREY'S STEP-BY-STEP COOKING

serves 4 | The mushrooms in this recipe are eaten raw, so it is essential to use very fresh unblemished ones. If you haven't any Japanese rice vinegar, use 3 tablespoons distilled white vinegar mixed with 1 tablespoon water and ¼ teaspoon sugar.

14	ounces large fresh mushrooms, preferably with 2-inch caps
5	scallions
3	tablespoons sake
2	tablespoons Japanese soy sauce *(shoyu)*
4	tablespoons Japanese rice vinegar
½	teaspoon salt

for garnish (optional)
Finely shredded scallion

1 Wipe the mushrooms with a damp cloth. If they are large, quarter them; otherwise, halve them. Finely chop the scallions.

2 Put the mushrooms and scallions in a bowl. Add all the remaining ingredients and toss to mix. Leave the mushrooms to marinate in their dressing for 5 minutes, then toss again and set aside for another 5 minutes.

3 Toss the mushrooms once more before serving, garnished with scallion shreds if you like.

The national drink in Japan is undoubtedly sake. These days, however, whisky or beer may be drunk right through a meal, and French wines, too, are encroaching.

For an informal meal, a family might serve grilled fish, a salad-like dish of spinach or beans dressed with sesame seeds, and perhaps carrots braised in stock or a dish of mushrooms. There would be soup, rice, pickles, and tea to round off the meal.

FOOD & WINE test-kitchen tips

- Lest you think the Japanese soy sauce called for in this recipe is difficult to find, you should know that the regular all-purpose soy sauce in the supermarket is Japanese. Kikkoman is a good brand.

- These mushrooms would make a nice, light first course too.

cucumber salad
dua leo ngam giam

from PLEASURES OF THE VIETNAMESE TABLE

serves 4 | The Vietnamese love cucumber and use it as an all-purpose vegetable. Sometimes the cucumbers are just cut into thin rounds and served plain; other times they're dressed in a sweet-and-sour dressing like this one. This refreshing salad goes well with grilled and steamed meats and seafood. It's even great with a bowl of fried rice. The preferred cucumber to use here is the baby version of the English cucumber, but any pickling variety will do. For interesting variations, sprinkle different herbs on top.

¼	cup rice or distilled white vinegar
1	tablespoon fresh lime juice
3	tablespoons sugar
½	teaspoon salt
6	pickling cucumbers, halved and cut into ⅛-inch-thick slices (about 2½ cups)
2	shallots, thinly sliced
½	serrano or other fresh chili, sliced (optional)
6	sprigs cilantro, chopped

1 Combine the vinegar, lime juice, sugar and salt in a bowl. Stir well and add the cucumbers, shallots, chili, if using, and cilantro. Set aside to stand for 15 minutes, then transfer to a bowl to serve.

FOOD & WINE test-kitchen tips

- We couldn't get pickling cucumbers when we tested this salad. English cucumbers worked just fine. They're the long, unwaxed ones that are usually sold shrink-wrapped.

- It's easy to get even, thin slices of cucumber by using an inexpensive plastic Japanese mandolin. Many food processors also do the job well.

- You might also consider serving this salad as one of several small plates before dinner—like Italian antipasti or Spanish tapas.

gratinéed asparagus and prosciutto
asparagi e prosciutto alla parmigiana

from BIBA'S TASTE OF ITALY | serves 6

Cooked green or white asparagus is bathed in melted butter, covered with freshly grated Parmigiano, and baked until the cheese is melted and a golden crust forms on top. Nothing could be simpler or more delicious—except perhaps this version, which has the addition of strips of prosciutto.

2 pounds asparagus

Salt

4 tablespoons ($^{1}/_{2}$ stick) unsalted butter

2 to 3 ounces thinly sliced prosciutto, cut into small strips

$^{1}/_{2}$ cup freshly grated Parmigiano-Reggiano

Cut off the tough ends of the asparagus. If the asparagus stalks are thick, peel them with a vegetable peeler or small sharp knife. Rinse the asparagus and arrange it in 1 or 2 bunches, securing them with rubber bands or kitchen string.

Bring 2 to 3 inches of water to a boil in an asparagus cooker or in a narrow stockpot over medium heat. Add a nice pinch of salt and stand the asparagus in the pot. Cover the top of the asparagus loosely with foil or with the cooker lid and cook until tender but still a bit crunchy to the bite (it will finish cooking in the oven), 3 to 8 minutes, depending on the thickness. Place a large bowl of ice water next to the stove. Remove the asparagus from the pot, remove the rubber bands or string, and place in the ice water to stop the cooking. Drain again, place on a clean kitchen towel, and pat dry. (The asparagus can be cooked to this point up to a day ahead. Cover tightly and refrigerate.)

▼

FOOD & WINE test-kitchen tips

- As the recipe suggests, this dish is good made with thin or thick asparagus. Contrary to what many people think, thick is just as tender as thin; the important thing is to choose spears of a similar size so they get done at the same time.

- Actually, this is in the antipasti section of *Biba's Taste of Italy*, and it makes a superb antipasto. But it's too good to save for four-course Italian dinners. Use the recipe also as a side dish with something simple, like roast chicken, or as a first course.

vegetables & side dishes

Preheat the oven to 400°F. Smear the bottom of a large baking dish with some of the butter.

Melt the remaining butter. Arrange a layer of the asparagus in the baking dish and season lightly with salt. Drizzle some of the melted butter over the asparagus, scatter the prosciutto over it, and sprinkle lightly with Parmigiano. Arrange another layer of asparagus on top and repeat as above, finishing with a generous sprinkling of cheese.

Place the baking dish on the middle rack of the oven and bake until the cheese has a nice golden color, 6 to 8 minutes. Remove from the oven and let stand for a few minutes before serving.

choosing and cooking asparagus Even though in some parts of the country asparagus is available most of the year, it is at its best in spring. When buying asparagus, look at the tips, which should be tightly closed, and their color, which should be a vivid green. Use asparagus as soon as you can; if you can't cook it right away, keep in the refrigerator, tightly wrapped, or stand the spears, just like flowers, in a vase with a few inches of water.

The method of cooking asparagus standing upright is typically Italian. While the thick asparagus stalks cook in the few inches of boiling water, the more delicate tips cook simultaneously in the steam above.

In this country, asparagus is usually cooked lying flat in a skillet of boiling water. If you use this method, make sure to keep the water to a gentle simmer so it won't break or damage the tips of the asparagus.

cauliflower with ginger and cilantro *gobi ki bhaji* india

from MADHUR JAFFREY'S STEP-BY-STEP COOKING

serves 6 to 8 | When an Indian housewife buys vegetables, the shopkeeper, if friendly, will often throw in a handful of green chilies and a bunch of fresh cilantro free. These two items are essential to Indian cooking and they are featured strongly here.

	2½- by 1-inch piece fresh ginger
1	large cauliflower
8	tablespoons vegetable oil
½	teaspoon ground turmeric
1	fresh hot green chili, finely sliced, or ¼ teaspoon cayenne pepper (optional)
1	cup (firmly packed) coarsely chopped fresh cilantro leaves
1	teaspoon ground cumin
2	teaspoons ground coriander
1	teaspoon garam masala
1	tablespoon lemon juice
	Salt

1 Peel and coarsely chop the ginger, then put into a blender with 4 tablespoons of water. Blend until smooth.

2 Cut off the thick, coarse stem of the cauliflower and remove all leaves. Break the cauliflower into florets with your hands, or a sharp knife if it is tightly packed. Slice the lower part of the stems into fairly thin rounds, then cut the cauliflower into slim delicate florets—no wider than 1 inch, with stems no longer than 1½ inches. Wash the florets and stem slices in a colander and leave to drain.

3 Heat the oil in a large frying pan over medium heat. Add the ginger paste and turmeric, and fry, stirring constantly, for about 2 minutes. Add the green chili or cayenne, and cilantro. Cook, stirring, for another 2 minutes.

▼

FOOD & WINE test-kitchen tips

- For Western-style meals, this makes an interesting side dish to accompany plain roasted or grilled chicken, pork, or beef. Or serve the cauliflower with Indian bread for an unusual first course. With lentils and rice, it becomes a whole dinner.

- You'll probably need about ¾ teaspoon salt for seasoning.

4   Add the cauliflower and continue to cook, stirring, for 5 minutes. (If the mixture begins to stick to the pan, sprinkle with 1 teaspoon warm water from time to time.)

5   Add the cumin, coriander, garam masala, lemon juice, salt, and 3 tablespoons warm water. Cook, stirring, for 3 to 4 minutes. Cover the pan, lower the heat, and cook slowly for 35 to 40 minutes, stirring gently every 10 minutes. The cauliflower is ready when it is tender with just a faint trace of crispness along its inner spine.

6   Transfer to a shallow serving bowl. Serve with hot chapatis, or parathas, or any kind of lentil dish and plain boiled rice.

Indian vegetable markets are an absolute delight to the eye and a source of great anticipatory glee to the palate. India produces most of the vegetables and fruit found here and many more but, of course, everything is seasonal. For example, you can expect to buy corn from August through to October, mangoes in the summer, cauliflower in the winter, and fresh mushrooms only during the humid monsoons. As a consequence, Indian menus change considerably with the seasons.

melanzane parmigiana
eggplant with parmesan cheese

from DA SILVANO COOKBOOK | serves 4

You can make this dish with large eggplant, but I like the way the small ones provide bite-size pieces.

4   small Italian eggplants (2½ to 3 oz/70 to 85g each)
½   cup/55g all-purpose flour
Fine sea salt
Freshly ground black pepper
¾ to 1 cup/175 to 225ml olive oil
1   cup/225ml *Sugo di Pomodoro* (page 195)
½   cup/55g freshly grated Parmigiano-Reggiano

Preheat the oven to 400°F/200°C/gas 6.

Slice the eggplants crosswise into ¼-inch/0.5-cm-thick slices.

Season the flour with salt and pepper and spread it out on a clean, dry surface. Press the eggplant slices into the flour, coating them on both sides.

Warm 4 tablespoons of the olive oil in a wide sauté pan over medium heat. Add a third to half of the eggplant slices to the pan in a single layer and cook until they are golden brown on the bottom, about 3 minutes. Flip the slices and brown on the other side, 2 to 3 minutes. Remove to paper towels to drain. Repeat once or twice, adding 4 tablespoons of olive oil to the pan and heating it before each batch of eggplant, until all the eggplant slices have been browned and drained.

▼

FOOD & WINE test-kitchen tips

- To season the ½ cup of flour, we used 2 teaspoons salt and ¼ teaspoon pepper. That's generous, but it's the only seasoning that the eggplant slices get before browning.

- Perhaps it's heretical to suggest this, but we think Japanese eggplant would be great in this recipe.

Pour 1 tablespoon olive oil into the bottom of a small ovenproof casserole and tilt and rotate the casserole to coat the bottom with the oil. Arrange a layer of eggplant on the bottom of the casserole. Cover with ¼ cup/55ml of the *sugo* and 2 tablespoons of the Parmigiano. Repeat twice with the remaining eggplant, sauce, and cheese, finishing with ½ cup/110ml tomato sauce and ¼ cup/30g Parmigiano.

Cover the casserole with foil and place it in the preheated oven. Bake for 15 minutes, then remove the foil and bake another 5 minutes to brown the Parmigiano.

Let rest for 5 minutes, then serve.

sugo di pomodoro tomato sauce | **makes about 2½ cups/560g** | This is the basic tomato sauce that we use in other recipes at Da Silvano, and throughout the book. If you want to make enough for a big group, or keep some extra in the freezer, the recipe multiplies very well.

- ¼ cup/55ml olive oil
- 4 cloves garlic, smashed and peeled
- 6 tablespoons fresh basil leaves (loosely packed)
- 2 cups/450g plum tomatoes, peeled and roughly chopped, or 1 can (28 oz/800g) peeled plum tomatoes from Italy, in their juice, crushed by hand

Fine sea salt
Freshly ground black pepper

Warm the olive oil in a pot large enough to hold all the ingredients over medium heat. Add 2 cloves of the garlic and cook until lightly browned, about 3 minutes. Remove and discard the cloves using tongs or a slotted spoon.

Remove the pot from the heat and toss in the basil leaves and the remaining 2 cloves of garlic. Add the tomatoes and return the pot to the heat. Season with salt and pepper and stir. Cook over low heat for about 15 minutes.

Use the sauce right away or let it cool and store it in an airtight container in the refrigerator for up to 3 days or freeze for up to 2 months.

cipolle al forno
weary onions from **SOFFRITTO**

serves 6 | This dish is not particularly difficult to prepare, but it requires great attention, especially in the cooking. This operation would ideally require a wood oven, or at least a good ordinary oven with steam injection. The onion quality is important. They should be red, not very dry, sugary, and of medium size. If you are able to find the type called Tropea, after the town near Naples where they are grown, they are the best. This dish can be served as a first course, as a side dish with every kind of meat, or however you like, hot or cold.

6   red onions, peeled and halved crosswise
Salt
Freshly ground black pepper
1   tablespoon chopped fresh oregano, or 1 teaspoon dried
1   cup (250 ml) extra virgin olive oil
1   cup (250 ml) dry red wine
1 to 2 cups (250 to 500 ml) meat stock, water, or red wine (optional)
Tuscan-style bread, for serving (see page 198)

Cut the bottom off each onion half to make a base, and set them upright in a baking pan. Sprinkle them with some salt and pepper and the oregano, and pour the oil and wine over them.

So far so good, and simple. The tricky part arises with baking. The aim is to have well-cooked onions, soft enough to melt in the mouth, but they should also taste totally different from boiled or stewed onions. The dish must taste of baked onions and, to that end, two or sometimes even three stages of baking are required. Put the pan in the oven heated to 400°F (250°C), and brown the onions for 30 minutes. Then reduce the heat to 250°F (125°C) and bake for 30 minutes or so, using steam set at half the full setting if you are lucky enough to have a baker's oven with a steam-injection system, or else covering the baking dish tightly with aluminum foil to keep the moisture in. During the baking, test the onions with a fork. When they are fully soft, they are ready. At the end of baking, 10 minutes of high heat 400°F (250°C) may again be required, both to give a good final browning of the onions and to condense somewhat the juices formed during baking. Throughout the time the onions are in the oven, you should frequently check the level of liquid, which must never dry out completely. If necessary, pour in some stock, water, or red wine. The name of the recipe suggests the look of the onions at the end of baking. In addition to being much reduced in volume, they should be squat and soft and look as if they are very tired.

▼

Let the dish rest for about 15 minutes before serving with abundant fresh white bread to soak up the cooking juice, formed by the oil, wine, and onion juices.

tuscan-style bread Tuscan loaves are large and round or elongated, with a golden crust and a soft white interior. They are made without salt or fat, leavened with natural yeast, and baked in loaves of about 2 pounds (1 kg). Outside of the region, many bakeries produce Tuscan-style bread under names such as *boule*, peasant, *paesano*, Italian country, and the like, with varying degrees of success. This kind of bread should never be purchased sliced as this will cause it to dry out and lose its flavor.

FOOD & WINE test-kitchen tips

- The onions should be about 2$\frac{1}{2}$ inches in diameter. If yours are larger, cook them longer.

- This dish reheats well. We were as happy with it the second day as the first.

polenta marbled with beans

from A NEW WAY TO COOK

serves 8 | I learned this unusual polenta dish from chef Piero Ferrini at La Cucina al Focolare, a cooking school in Tuscany. Piero folded local borlotti beans into warm polenta and molded it into a loaf that he sliced and fried to make crisp, marbelized slabs.

$\frac{1}{3}$ cup (2$\frac{1}{2}$ ounces) borlotti or cranberry beans,
      picked over and rinsed

6   garlic cloves, lightly smashed, tissuey skin removed

5   large sage leaves

2   teaspoons kosher salt, or more to taste

1$\frac{1}{2}$ cups coarse polenta

4$\frac{1}{2}$ cups cold water

$\frac{1}{3}$ cup (1 ounce) finely grated aged pecorino Toscano,
      Fiore Sardo, or Parmigiano-Reggiano cheese

Freshly ground black pepper

1   tablespoon plus 1 teaspoon extra-virgin olive oil

Soak the beans overnight in a medium heavy saucepan with enough water to cover by 3 inches. Drain and add fresh water to cover by 3 inches, along with the garlic and sage. Simmer until the beans are just tender but not falling apart, about 1 hour; season with $\frac{1}{2}$ teaspoon of the salt after 30 minutes. Replenish the water as necessary so that the beans have plenty of water to cook in. Drain the beans and discard the garlic and sage.

In a large heavy saucepan, combine the polenta, water, and the remaining 1$\frac{1}{2}$ teaspoons salt. Bring to a boil over high heat, stirring constantly. Reduce the heat to medium and cook, stirring frequently, until very thick and it pulls away from the sides and bottom of the pan, about 25 minutes. Stir in the cheese and pepper to taste. Adjust the seasonings, then gently fold in the beans with a spatula, being careful not to break the beans.

▼

FOOD & WINE test-kitchen tips

- To slice the polenta neatly, hold the blade of your knife under hot water, dry it, and cut. The heat will help your knife slide right through.

- With the addition of tomato or another sauce, this polenta can become a main dish. The recipe will then serve four.

Vegetables & side dishes

199

Spoon the mixture into a 4-by-8½-inch loaf pan or two 3½-by-5½-inch mini-loaf pans, pressing down with the back of a spoon to remove any air pockets. Cool to room temperature, cover, and refrigerate until completely firm, about 1 hour. Unmold the polenta and cut into ½-inch-thick slices.

Heat 2 large nonstick skillets over medium heat. Add half the oil to each and swirl to coat. Arrange the slices in the pans. Fry them for 2 to 3 minutes on each side until golden and crisp, adding more oil as necessary. (Alternatively, you can brush the slices with the oil and grill them over hot coals.) Serve hot.

in advance   You can prepare the beans up to 2 days ahead and store, covered, in the refrigerator. You can assemble the loaf up to 2 days ahead and store, covered, in the refrigerator.

scallion noodles *mi kho hanh*

from PLEASURES OF THE VIETNAMESE TABLE

serves 4 as a side dish | It seems like there's a version of this noodle dish everywhere in Asia. Originally from China, it calls for tossing fresh egg noodles with oil that's been infused with scallions. It can be served as a snack by itself or as a wonderful accompaniment to grilled meats such as Grilled Five-Spice Chicken (page 163) or crab dishes.

1   bunch scallions

3   tablespoons vegetable oil

2   shallots, thinly sliced

2   tablespoons soy sauce or to taste

Pinch salt

1   pound fresh egg noodles, boiled 2 to 3 minutes,
    rinsed and drained

1   Remove the white part of the scallions and cut into thin rings. Cut the green part into 2-inch lengths and set aside.

2   Heat the oil in a large nonstick skillet over moderate heat. Add the shallots and the white and green parts of the scallions. Stir until fragrant, about 1 minute. Add the soy sauce, salt and noodles. Stir gently, being careful not to break the noodles. Turn several times so the noodles are coated evenly with the oil and are thoroughly heated. Transfer to a serving plate and serve immediately.

FOOD & WINE test-kitchen tips

- Fresh Italian egg pasta is very similar to Asian egg noodles. The Italian version worked well in this dish.

- If you leave the scallions whole, rather than separating the bulbs from the leaves, it'll be easier to cut the white parts into thin rounds. You can hold on to the greens and slice right up to the point where they start.

puré di patate
potato purée **from SOFFRITTO**

serves 6 | In Tuscany, this purée, although made of potatoes, is considered a formal side dish. It is essentially mashed potatoes lavishly enriched with a lot of butter and Parmesan cheese, and it is usually served with substantial meat courses, roasts, or stews. The dish looks simple, but it is not; it requires a lot of care and some practice to get the right consistency. It is essential that all ingredients are added when the purée is hot, otherwise it will never be smooth enough. You may need to practice making it several times, critically examining the results, before you feel you have mastered it. Note that the quantities given should be taken as approximate, as they vary considerably with the potato quality.

2	pounds (1 kg) boiling potatoes
2	cups (500 ml) milk
Salt	
7	tablespoons (100 g) unsalted butter
2	cups (250 g) grated Parmesan cheese

Wash the potatoes, put them in a pot of cold water, and boil for about 20 minutes, probing them from time to time with a fork. Once you are satisfied that the potatoes are cooked inside, drain them, and peel them as soon as they are cool enough to handle. Heat the milk in a small pan, taking care not to boil it. Pour half of the warm milk into a pot large enough to hold the potatoes. Reserve the remaining milk, keeping it warm over a very low flame—again, be careful not to scorch it. Put the potatoes through a food mill directly into the pot of warm milk. Set the pot on a very low flame and stir continuously with a wooden spoon for about 5 minutes. Add salt to taste.

A good potato purée must not be too thick, so add more milk, continuing to stir, until you think the purée is the right consistency. Taste for salt, then add the butter and Parmesan. Take the pot off the stove and keep stirring until the butter has melted and mixed in well. Should you need to reheat the purée, put it in a bain-marie or double boiler over low heat, always stirring it with a wooden spoon. Serve hot.

FOOD & WINE test-kitchen tips

- If you don't have a food mill, you might try a ricer. No ricer either? Mash the potatoes very thoroughly. It would be a shame to skip this recipe due to lack of equipment.

- The recipe suggests that you taste for salt at two different points in the cooking. Do so carefully. We found that despite the Parmesan, we needed about ¾ teaspoon salt altogether.

gratin dauphinoise

from ONE POTATO TWO POTATO | serves 6 to 8

There is much said and written about the correct way to make the ultimate gratin. Some add eggs to help thicken; some abhor the addition of cheese; others insist on simmering the potato slices first in milk, draining them, and adding fresh cream for baking. We like our version—simple enough to make and marvelously rich. While we use a bit more cream than milk, you can just as well prepare this with any combination of the two, as long as you come up with 2½ cups—enough to just cover the potatoes. Never worry about making too much of this, because a cold slice of gratin is one of the best breakfasts we can imagine.

2   pounds Yukon Gold or russet potatoes,
     peeled and very thinly sliced
Coarse salt and freshly ground white pepper
1   cup milk
1½ cups heavy cream
3   ounces Gruyère cheese, shredded
     (about ¾ cup)

Heat the oven to 375 degrees. Place a sheet of heavy-duty aluminum foil on the rack under the one you'll be baking the gratin on. Gratins can make a serious mess when they spill over. Butter a large gratin dish or a 3-quart flameproof casserole dish.

Arrange the potatoes in the dish in overlapping layers, sprinkling with salt and pepper as you go.

Combine the milk and cream and pour it over the potatoes. Heat the dish over medium-high heat until the cream begins to simmer. Watch carefully so that it doesn't boil over and make a real mess.

▼

FOOD & WINE test-kitchen tips

- A mandolin, either a metal French or a plastic Japanese one, makes quick work of slicing the potatoes ever so thin.

- It's easy to lose track of seasoning when you're layering a dish like this. We used 1 teaspoon of salt in all for the 2 pounds of potatoes, and ¼ teaspoon pepper (black is fine if you don't have white).

Sprinkle the cheese on top and bake until the top is very brown and bubbly, about 40 minutes. Because of the cheese, the surface of this gratin will get quite brown. Don't chicken out and remove it from the oven before the potatoes are completely tender and the edges of the gratin look as if the cream has broken.

Let the gratin sit for about 10 minutes before serving.

potato, leek, and bacon panfry from ONE POTATO TWO POTATO

serves 4 | Here's another great idea from Tom Colicchio, chef-owner of Craft restaurant and Gramercy Tavern in New York City. Not quite hash, not quite home fries: what it is, is delicious. If you can find them, try German Butterballs in this dish.

1/4	pound thick-cut bacon
2	tablespoons unsalted butter
4	heaping cups sliced leeks
	(white and light green parts of about 4 leeks)

Coarse salt and freshly ground white pepper

2	tablespoons vegetable oil
1	pound yellow-fleshed potatoes,
	scrubbed and sliced 1/16 inch thick
1	tablespoon chopped fresh thyme

Cut the bacon into matchsticks. Put it in a large skillet with 1 tablespoon of the butter and cook over medium heat until the bacon has rendered its fat but has not browned. Add the leeks, season with salt and white pepper, and cook until the leeks have begun to soften, about 5 minutes. Stir often while the leeks are cooking, and transfer the leeks and bacon to a bowl when they're done.

Spoon the oil into the skillet and heat it until it shimmers. Add the potatoes, the remaining 1 tablespoon butter, and salt and pepper to taste and cook until the potatoes are tender, 20 to 25 minutes. They will stick some and become translucent; stir with a metal spoon or spatula. Add the thyme, the leeks and bacon, and 1/4 cup water and cook, stirring frequently, until the leeks and potatoes are very tender and the flavors have melded, about another 5 minutes. Serve hot.

FOOD & WINE test-kitchen tips

- If you can't get fresh thyme, parsley is a better substitute than dried thyme.

- We used black pepper rather than the suggested white and found the dish came to no harm.

desserts

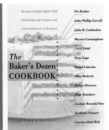

brown sugar thins

from THE BAKER'S DOZEN COOKBOOK

makes about 7 dozen cookies | Ideal for making cut-out cookies with children (the dough is so forgiving that it can be rolled out repeatedly), this is an easy recipe with a rich brown sugar flavor. Because it contains more molasses, you'll get more pronounced flavor with dark brown sugar, but you can use light brown if you wish.—JULIA COOKENBOO

2^1/$_4$ cups all-purpose flour

^{1}/$_4$ teaspoon salt

^{1}/$_2$ pound (2 sticks) unsalted butter, softened

1 cup packed dark brown sugar

1 teaspoon vanilla extract

1 Position racks in the center and top third of the oven and preheat to 300°F. Line two large baking sheets with parchment paper or lightly butter them.

2 Sift the flour and salt into a medium bowl; set aside.

3 In the bowl of a heavy-duty stand mixer fitted with the paddle attachment, beat the butter, brown sugar, and vanilla on medium speed until the mixture is light in color and texture, about 3 minutes. Reduce the speed to low and gradually add the flour mixture to make a smooth dough. Gather the dough into a smooth, flat disk.

4 Working with about one-fourth of the dough at a time, roll it out on a lightly floured work surface until ^{1}/$_8$ inch thick. Do not use too much flour. Occasionally turn the dough or slide a long metal spatula under it to be sure that it isn't sticking. Using a soft pastry brush, brush off any excess flour from the surface of the dough.

▼

FOOD & WINE test-kitchen tips

- Any electric beater will work here; you don't have to have the kind with a paddle attachment.

- Try using several different cookie cutters for a variety of shapes.

creaming butter and sugar

Cut the butter into small pieces and place in the bowl with the sugar. Start creaming the butter on medium speed for about a minute to initiate the aeration, then gradually beat in the sugar. Continue beating, scraping down the sides and bottom of the bowl every minute or so to incorporate every bit of butter and sugar into the creamed mixture. This will take 4 to 7 minutes with a heavy-duty mixer. When thoroughly creamed, the mixture will look like the photo above.

5 Using a cookie cutter dipped in flour, cut out the cookies, starting at the edges of the rolled-out dough and working your way into the center (this minimizes waste). Arrange the cookies about 1 inch apart on the prepared sheets. Gather up the scraps and briefly knead together. Let stand for about 5 minutes before rolling out again.

6 Bake, switching the position of the sheets from top to bottom and front to back halfway through baking, until the cookies are a shade deeper brown than the raw dough, about 15 minutes. Cool on the sheets for 3 minutes, then transfer to wire cooling racks and cool completely. (The cookies can be stored at room temperature in an airtight container for up to 5 days.)

baker's notes The dough can be prepared, tightly wrapped in plastic wrap, and refrigerated for up to 5 days. Let it come to room temperature before rolling out. If the dough cracks during rolling, it is too cold; let it stand for a few more minutes, then try again.

Dipping the cookie cutter in flour every time you cut out a cookie helps release the dough from the cutter.

Be sure to brush excess flour off the dough before cutting. Use a soft brush, as stiff bristles could scrape the dough.

double walnut meltaways

from FEARLESS BAKING | makes about 31 cookies

Baking these powdered sugar–coated walnut and butter cookies is an any-holiday-that-comes-along tradition at our house. No holiday in the offing? We make them anyway. I've tasted many versions of these cookies, but never ones like these that include both ground and chopped walnuts. The ground walnuts create the melting texture, while the chopped walnuts supply the distinct walnut flavor. You're probably familiar with these sugar-dusted cookies as the ones that disappear first from any cookie table.

baking answers A food processor works well for preparing the ground walnuts, but it's easiest to control the size of the chopped walnuts by using a knife to cut them.

In addition to cookie balls, these cookies can be formed into crescent or ring shapes. For crescents, roll a rounded teaspoon of dough between the palms of your hands into a cylinder with tapered ends and curve it to form a crescent. For rings, roll the rounded teaspoon of dough between the palms of your hands into a rope about 4 inches long and press the ends together to form a circle. The baking time remains the same.

a step ahead The cooled cookies can be frozen for up to 2 months. Place the bottoms of 2 cookies together and wrap them carefully in plastic wrap. Put the wrapped cookies in a metal or plastic freezer container and cover tightly. Label with the date and contents. Defrost the wrapped cookies at room temperature.

necessities 1 heavyweight baking sheet and 1 wire rack for cooling the cookies

1	cup unbleached all-purpose flour
1/4	teaspoon baking powder
1/4	teaspoon salt
1/2	teaspoon ground cinnamon
1/4	pound (1 stick) soft unsalted butter
1/4	cup powdered sugar
1	teaspoon vanilla extract
1/2	cup ground walnuts
1/4	cup coarsely chopped walnuts
1	cup powdered sugar, sifted, for coating the cookies

mix the dough

Position an oven rack in the middle of the oven. Preheat the oven to 300°F. Line a baking sheet with parchment paper. It is not necessary to butter the paper.

Stir the flour, baking powder, salt, and cinnamon together in a small bowl and set aside.

Put the butter, powdered sugar, and vanilla in a large bowl and beat with an electric mixer on medium speed until the mixture looks smooth and creamy, about 1 minute. Move the beaters around in the bowl if using a handheld electric mixer. Stop the mixer and scrape the mixture from the sides of the bowl and any that becomes caught in the beaters as needed throughout the mixing process. Decrease the speed to low and add the flour mixture, mixing just until it is incorporated and a smooth dough forms. Add the ground and chopped walnuts, mixing just to distribute them evenly.

Roll a rounded teaspoon of dough between the palms of your hands into 1-inch balls. Place them about 1½ inches apart on the baking sheet. Or, roll the dough into a cylinder with tapered ends and curve each cookie into a crescent. The cookies do not spread a lot during baking.

bake and serve the cookies

Bake until the bottoms are light brown, about 30 minutes. Cool the cookies on the baking sheet for 5 minutes. Use a thin metal spatula to transfer the cookies to a wire rack to cool completely. Put the sifted powdered sugar in a shallow dish or pie tin and roll each cookie in it until evenly coated. The cookies can be stored at room temperature, tightly sealed in a metal tin, for up to 5 days.

FOOD & WINE test-kitchen tips

- If you don't have parchment paper, grease the baking sheets. That'll work just fine.

- These cookies are as irresistible made with pecans as with walnuts.

almond and chocolate sandwich cookies

from THE BAKER'S DOZEN COOKBOOK

makes 40 cookies | These crisp cookies are a fine accompaniment to ice cream. We bet they'll remind you of a popular and very expensive supermarket cookie (that will go unnamed). Allow time for the dough to chill.—JULIA COOKENBOO

1	cup whole natural almonds, toasted and cooled (see page 217)
3/4	cup plus 3 tablespoons sugar
3/4	cup all-purpose flour
1	teaspoon baking powder
1/8	teaspoon salt
8	tablespoons (1 stick) unsalted butter, softened
1	large egg
1/4	teaspoon almond extract
4	ounces semisweet or bittersweet chocolate, finely chopped

1 In a food processor fitted with the chopping blade, process the almonds with 3 tablespoons of the sugar until the almonds are finely ground. Set aside.

2 Sift the flour, baking powder, and salt onto a sheet of wax paper or into a bowl. Set aside.

3 In the bowl of a heavy-duty stand mixer fitted with the paddle attachment, beat the butter with the remaining 3/4 cup sugar on medium speed until the mixture is light in color and texture, at least 3 minutes. Beat in the egg and almond extract, then the almond mixture, blending just until smooth. On low speed, gradually beat in the flour mixture just until smooth.

4 Cover the dough tightly with plastic wrap. Refrigerate until the dough is thoroughly chilled, at least 2 hours or up to 5 days.

▼

FOOD & WINE test-kitchen tips

- In case you don't have the kind of mixer with a paddle attachment, rest assured that beaters are the equivalent in other models.

- We liked these cookies sprinkled with confectioners' sugar.

215

5   Position racks in the center and top third of the oven and preheat to 350°F. Line two large baking sheets with parchment paper or lightly butter them.

6   Using 1 teaspoon for each, portion the dough into 80 pieces. Put 2 pieces of dough into one hand and roll between your palms into 2 balls. (This may seem a bit odd at first, but it works, and cuts the work time in half.) Place the balls about 1½ inches apart on the prepared baking sheets. Do not crowd them, as they will spread during baking. (You will probably have to bake these cookies on three sheets.)

7   Bake, switching the position of the sheets from top to bottom and front to back halfway through baking, until the cookies are lightly browned all over, 10 to 12 minutes.

8   Let the cookies cool on the sheets for 3 minutes. Carefully transfer to wire cooling racks and cool completely.

9   In the top part of a double boiler over hot, not simmering, water, melt the chocolate. Using a small icing spatula, spread about ½ teaspoon on the underside of a cookie, then sandwich with another cookie, placing them back to back. Refrigerate briefly to set the chocolate. (The cookies can be stored at room temperature in an airtight container for up to 5 days.)

baker's note   For a fancier-looking cookie, lightly brush the top of each cookie with an egg glaze (beat 1 egg with 1 teaspoon water) and top with a few sliced almonds before baking. Even without the chocolate filling, these are excellent wafer-type cookies.

toasting nuts   Toasting brings out the flavor of all nuts and is required to remove the skins from hazelnuts. (Skinned, but untoasted, hazelnuts are now available at many markets, and while they are a boon, some bakers miss the toasted flavor.) To toast nuts, spread them on a baking sheet. Bake in a preheated 350°F oven for about 10 minutes, stirring often, until the nuts are fragrant and lightly toasted to a pale golden brown.

caramel pecan cookie
sandwich hearts

from FEARLESS BAKING

makes seven 3-inch cookie sandwiches | Two hearts beat as one in these brown sugar and pecan cookie sandwiches filled with caramel and pecans. I cut the cookies into 3-inch dessert-size hearts, but smaller or other versions cut into hearts, stars, or rounds are equally good choices. The caramel filling used for these cookies is a slightly thicker mixture than caramel sauce.

baking answers I grind the pecans for the cookies in a food processor and process them up to the point that some small pieces of pecans, about ⅛ inch in size, remain among the ground nuts.

Rolling the dough between 2 pieces of wax paper prevents the dough from sticking to the rolling surface and makes it easy to cut and transfer the cookies to the baking sheet. By using the wax paper, the dough can be re-rolled several times without additional chilling.

I find the easiest way to caramelize sugar is to dissolve the sugar in some water by cooking the mixture over a low heat to melt the sugar, then raising the heat and boiling it until it turns an evenly dark golden color. Cooking the sugar with some water helps the sugar melt evenly. The sugar caramelizes as the water evaporates and the sugar mixture reaches a temperature of over 320°F. As the sugar mixture boils and becomes hotter, the boiling bubbles change from large bubbles to tiny bubbles, to almost none or a very few bubbles. The change in the bubbles signals the sugar is about to reach the caramel stage. It takes about 10 minutes to reach this dark golden–colored stage, but as soon as the color begins to change, the process goes quickly, so watch it constantly. You can drop a bit of caramel on a light-colored plate to test the color, then remove the caramel from the heat as soon as the color you want is reached. Remember, the only way you can ruin caramel is to burn it. Any hard sugar crystals that form as the mixture cooks will dissolve in the hot caramel at the end of the cooking process.

Once the sugar caramelizes, remove the pan from the heat and slowly add warm cream to the hot caramel. This produces caramel sauce or a caramel filling. The more cream that is added, the thinner the finished sauce. When the warm cream is added to the hot caramelized sugar, the mixture bubbles up, so be careful that it does not splash on you. That is why you want to add the cream slowly and use a large saucepan to cook caramelized sugar that will have a warm liquid added to it.

Use a wooden spoon to stir the caramel. It will not retain heat and become too hot to handle as a metal spoon can.

necessities 1 heavyweight baking sheet, a rolling pin, 1 wire rack for cooling the cookies, a heart-shaped cookie cutter that is about 3 inches long, or cookie cutters of your choice, and a heavy 3-quart saucepan

pecan cookies
- $^3/_4$ cup plus 2 tablespoons unbleached all-purpose flour
- 2 tablespoons cornstarch
- $^1/_4$ teaspoon salt
- $^1/_2$ teaspoon ground cinnamon
- $^1/_4$ pound (1 stick) soft unsalted butter
- $^1/_3$ cup packed light brown sugar
- 1 teaspoon vanilla extract
- $^1/_2$ cup coarsely ground pecans, largest pieces about $^1/_8$ inch
- 3 tablespoons finely chopped pecans, about $^1/_4$ inch in size

caramel filling
- $^1/_3$ cup whipping cream
- $^1/_4$ cup water
- $^1/_2$ cup granulated sugar
- $^1/_4$ cup finely chopped pecans

Powdered sugar for dusting the top of the cookie sandwiches

mix the dough

Position the oven rack in the middle of the oven. Preheat the oven to 325°F. Line a baking sheet with parchment paper.

Sift the flour, cornstarch, salt, and cinnamon together onto a piece of wax paper or into a medium bowl and set aside.

▼

Put the butter, brown sugar, and vanilla in a large bowl and beat with an electric mixer on medium speed for about 1 minute until the mixture looks smooth. Move the beaters around in the bowl if using a handheld electric mixer. Stop the mixer and scrape the mixture from the sides of the bowl and any that becomes caught in the beaters as needed throughout the mixing process. Decrease the speed to low and mix in the ground pecans. Add the flour mixture, mixing just until no loose flour shows and the dough holds together in large clumps and pulls away from the sides of the bowl. Gather the dough into a ball, then press it into a disk about 6 inches in diameter. Wrap the dough in plastic wrap and chill it in the refrigerator for about 40 minutes until it is cool and firm, but soft enough to roll. The chilled dough should not be so hard that you can't press your finger into it. The dough can chill overnight, but it will need to soften at room temperature for at least 1 hour to become soft enough to roll.

Put the dough between 2 large pieces of wax paper. Roll the dough from the center out to about a 12-inch circle that is 1/8 inch thick. Carefully peel off the top piece of wax paper. Use a 3-inch-long heart-shaped cookie cutter to cut out cookie hearts. Use a thin metal spatula to loosen the cookies from the wax paper and slide them onto the prepared baking sheet, placing them 1 inch apart. Press all of the dough scraps together to form a smooth ball of dough and repeat the rolling and cutting process between pieces of wax paper. If you still have a lot of scraps of dough, press them together and repeat the rolling and cutting for a third time. Each rolling produces a smaller circle of rolled dough and fewer cookies. Leaving about a 1/4-inch edge bare, sprinkle a generous teaspoon of chopped pecans onto the center of half of the cookies. Press them gently into the dough.

FOOD & WINE test-kitchen tips

- Do not be put off by the length of this recipe. It's not long because it's so complicated but because the directions are so thorough.

- If you don't have heavy baking sheets, double up: use 2 thin sheets stacked together.

bake the cookies

Bake the cookies for about 18 minutes until the tops have colored slightly, reversing the baking sheets after 10 minutes front to back and top to bottom to ensure that the cookies bake evenly. Gently touch a cookie and it will feel crusty on the outside. Be careful not to burn yourself. The cookie bottoms will be evenly golden. Cool the cookies for 5 minutes on the baking sheet. Use an offset metal spatula or wide spatula to transfer the cookies to a wire cake rack to cool thoroughly. The cookies become crisp as they cool.

cook the filling

Put the cream in a small saucepan and heat it over low heat. The cream should be hot, about 150°F. if measured with a food thermometer when it is added to the hot sugar mixture. Do not boil the cream. If the cream should boil and a skin forms on top, use a spoon to lift out the skin and discard it. Cook the water and granulated sugar to a caramel while keeping the cream hot over low heat.

Put the water and granulated sugar in a heavy-bottomed saucepan that has at least a 3-quart capacity. Cover and cook over low heat until the sugar dissolves, about 5 minutes. Stir the mixture occasionally to help the sugar dissolve. Remove the cover, increase the heat to medium-high, and bring to a boil. Do not worry if a few sugar crystals form on the side of the pan. Boil the mixture until the sugar melts, caramelizes, and turns a dark golden color, about 10 minutes. As the sugar reaches the caramel stage, the bubbles subside and become small. You can dip the spoon in the caramel and drop a drop on a light-colored plate to see the color. As soon as the mixture begins to turn golden, stir it with a wooden spoon once or twice to ensure that the sugar cooks evenly and that all of the sugar caramelizes. Once the caramel begins to change color, it reaches the dark golden stage quickly, so watch it constantly.

Remove the caramel from the heat. Slowly and carefully add the hot cream to the hot sugar. The mixture will bubble up, so be careful. Once the bubbles subside, if the caramel is sticking to the bottom or is not completely smooth, return the saucepan to low heat. Cook the caramel, stirring continuously with the wooden spoon, for 1 or 2 minutes until the caramel is completely dissolved and the mixture is smooth. Remove the pan from the heat and stir in the finely chopped pecans. Cool the caramel filling for about 1½ hours, until it is thick enough to spoon onto the cookies without running off them. The caramel filling can be cooled for about 15 minutes, poured into a heatproof container (a Pyrex-type measuring cup works well), and refrigerated for about 40 minutes to thicken.

▼

221

fill and serve the cookies

Turn the cookies without the pecan topping bottom side up. Leaving a ¼-inch edge bare, spread about 1 tablespoon of cooled caramel filling over these cookie bottoms. Press the remaining cookies, pecan side up, gently onto the caramel filling. Dust with powdered sugar and serve. The 3-inch cookie hearts can be served as individual desserts. The cookies can be covered and stored either at room temperature or in the refrigerator for up to 4 days. Serve cold or at room temperature.

applesauce gingerbread

from THE BAKER'S DOZEN COOKBOOK

makes about 10 servings | Applesauce gives this spicy gingerbread its moist texture. If you wish, add ½ cup dried cranberries or raisins to the batter. Note that the cake doesn't rise much; it is the height of a single layer cake.—CAROLYN B. WEIL

cake

2	cups all-purpose flour
1	teaspoon baking soda
1	teaspoon ground ginger
½	teaspoon ground cinnamon
½	teaspoon ground cloves
½	teaspoon freshly grated nutmeg
½	teaspoon salt
1	cup packed light brown sugar
½	cup vegetable oil
1	large egg, at room temperature
½	cup applesauce
½	cup water
3	tablespoons finely chopped crystallized ginger

glaze

1	cup confectioners' sugar
2	tablespoons fresh orange juice, or as needed

1 Position a rack in the center of the oven and preheat to 350°F. Lightly spray a 10-inch tube (angel food) pan with nonstick spray.

2 To make the cake, sift the flour, baking soda, ginger, cinnamon, cloves, nutmeg, and salt into a large bowl.

▼

FOOD & WINE test-kitchen tips

- Run a knife between the edge of the gingerbread and the pan before unmolding.

- Flavor the glaze with lemon juice rather than orange if you prefer.

3 In another large bowl, whisk the brown sugar, oil, and egg until well combined, then whisk in the applesauce and water. Add the dry ingredients and stir well. Fold in the ginger. Spread evenly in the prepared pan.

4 Bake until the top is firm and springs back when pressed with your fingers, about 35 minutes.

5 Transfer to a wire cooling rack and cool completely in the pan. Remove the cake from the pan.

6 To make the glaze, sift the confectioners' sugar into a small bowl. Stir in enough of the orange juice to make a glaze about the consistency of heavy cream. Drizzle the glaze over the top of the cake, letting the excess drip down the sides. Let stand to set the glaze. (The cake can be stored at room temperature for up to 3 days, wrapped in plastic wrap.)

semolina cake from LA BELLA CUCINA

serves 6 | A wonderful "keeping" cake, this is very moist and tender—really a cross between a cake and a pudding—and good for snacking on any time of the day.

To dress it up for dessert, use rum instead of orange flower water, add homemade or finest quality finely diced candied orange and citron rind in place of the orange zest, and, as a final touch, add a sprinkling of natural green pistachios.

If desired, dust the top with confectioners' sugar just before serving.

Unsalted butter and semolina for the springform pan

4   cups milk

Small pinch of sea salt

$^3/_4$ cup semolina

1$^1/_3$ cups sugar

2   tablespoons orange blossom water

Grated zest of 2 oranges, preferably organic

4   eggs, lightly beaten

Heat the oven to 375 degrees. Butter an 8-inch springform pan. Sprinkle with some semolina and shake out the excess.

Place the milk and salt in a saucepan. Bring the milk to the brink of a boil over low heat. Add the semolina in a thin stream, whisking continuously with a sturdy wire whisk. Continue until the semolina thickens and begins to pull away from the sides of the pan.

Remove from the heat and continue stirring for 1 or 2 minutes. Let cool a little. Stir in the sugar. Add the orange blossom water and orange zest and stir until evenly distributed. Quickly stir in the beaten eggs.

Pour into the pan. Bake for 1 hour or until firm to the touch and lightly brown on top.

Remove from the oven and cool on a rack to room temperature.

Refrigerate to firm up the cake, about 30 minutes. Unmold. Serve cool or at room temperature. Store cake in refrigerator wrapped in waxed paper.

FOOD & WINE test-kitchen tips

- Be sure to get coarse semolina, not semolina flour, for this cake.

- The cake keeps well—wrapped and refrigerated—for 2 days.

hazelnut chocolate
meringue with blackberries

serves 8 to 10 | In northern California fabulous blackberries can often be had right up to Labor Day. I celebrate the last days of summer with a backyard barbecue and this informal dessert.

ingredients

meringue

5 ounces bittersweet or semisweet chocolate, chopped, or $^3/_4$ cup semisweet chocolate chips

$^1/_2$ cup hazelnuts, toasted and skinned and chopped medium fine

$^2/_3$ cup sugar

3 egg whites

$^1/_8$ teaspoon cream of tartar

filling

1 cup heavy cream

$^1/_2$ teaspoon vanilla extract

1 tablespoon sugar

$1^1/_2$ pints blackberries, rinsed and spread out to dry on paper towels

equipment

Baking sheet, lined with parchment paper

Pastry bag

Plain pastry tip with a $^1/_2$-inch opening (Ateco #806 or #807) (optional)

Position a rack in the center of the oven. Preheat the oven to 300°F.

To make the chocolate meringue, using a heavy pencil line, trace one 9-inch circle or a 12 x 6-inch rectangle or any other shape of similar size on the baking pan liner. Turn the paper over so that pencil marks will not transfer to the meringue.

▼

FOOD & WINE test-kitchen tips

- To toast and skin the hazelnuts, put them in a pie plate and roast them for about 10 minutes; when the nuts are cool enough to handle, rub them together to remove the skins.

- The easiest way to form the meringue into a perfect round is to put a 9-inch cake ring on the parchment-lined baking sheet, spread the meringue, and lift the ring. Voilà.

Mix the chocolate with the nuts and half of the sugar. Set aside.

In a clean, dry mixing bowl, beat the egg whites and cream of tartar on medium speed until soft peaks form when the beaters are lifted. On high speed, gradually add the remaining sugar, about a tablespoon at a time, taking about 1 to 1½ minutes. The mixture should stand in stiff glossy peaks when the beaters are lifted. Use a rubber spatula to fold in the chocolate mixture, just until incorporated. If you are using a pastry bag, insert the plain round tip and scrape the meringue into the bag. Starting at the center of the traced circle, pipe an ever-widening spiral of meringue (counterclockwise if you are right-handed) to cover the entire circle. Pipe a raised border around the edge. Or scrape the meringue into the center of the traced circle. With the back of a large spoon, spread the meringue to form a shallow shell with slightly raised edges.

Bake 10 to 15 minutes, or until the meringue begins to turn golden. Turn the oven down to 200°F. and continue to bake for 2 hours. Cool the meringue in a turned-off oven. Cool completely before using or storing. *Meringues may be stored in an airtight container at least 2 months.*

In a chilled bowl with chilled beaters, beat the cream with the vanilla and sugar until nearly stiff. Fill the meringue shell with the whipped cream. Mound the berries on top. Refrigerate until serving.

fastest fudge cake

from A YEAR IN CHOCOLATE

serves 8 to 10 | Here's an emergency foolproof birthday or summer supper cake too good to save for an emergency. Don't even look for the mixer. I get the best results stirring with a rubber spatula or a wooden spoon. For speed, melt the butter in a large microwave-safe mixing bowl to eliminate a dirty pot, and make the frosting while the cake bakes.

ingredients

1 cup all-purpose flour

$1/4$ cup plus 2 tablespoons unsweetened natural cocoa powder

$1/2$ teaspoon baking soda

$1/4$ teaspoon salt

8 tablespoons melted unsalted butter, warm (1 stick)

$1 1/4$ cups (packed) brown sugar

2 eggs, cold or at room temperature

1 teaspoon vanilla extract

$1/2$ cup hot tap water

Fast Fudge Frosting (page 230)

equipment

8-inch square or 9-inch round cake pan

Position a rack in the lower third of the oven. Grease the bottom of the pan or line it with parchment paper. Preheat the oven to 350°F.

To make the cake, whisk the flour, cocoa, baking soda, and salt together. Sift only if the cocoa remains lumpy. Set aside.

In a large bowl, combine the warm melted butter and brown sugar. Add the eggs and vanilla and stir until well blended. Add all of the flour mixture at once. Using a rubber spatula or wooden spoon, stir only until all the flour is moistened. Pour the hot water over the batter all at once. Stir only until the water is incorporated and the batter is smooth. Scrape the batter into the pan.

▼

FOOD & WINE test-kitchen tips

- The dry ingredients for this cake are mixed together with a whisk—a great method that's frequently used by chefs. It's the quickest way to combine the dry ingredients in any recipe.

- For the smoothest, easiest frosting job, use a warm cake spatula (the long, skinny metal kind). Just dip it in hot water, dry, and spread. Repeat as often as necessary to keep the spatula warm.

Bake until a toothpick inserted in the center of the cake comes out clean, 25 to 30 minutes. Cool the cake in the pan on a rack for about 10 minutes before unmolding. To unmold, slide a slim knife around the edges of the cake to release it from the pan. Invert the cake and peel off the paper liner. Turn the cake right side up and cool it completely on a rack before frosting the top and sides. Or cool the cake in the pan and frost the top only.

fast fudge frosting | **makes 1²/₃ cups** | It's not only fast, it's versatile. Serve it warm over ice cream for a great sauce, dip cupcake tops, or pour it over a pound cake.

> 5   tablespoons unsalted butter
>
> ³/₄   cup sugar
>
> ²/₃   cup unsweetened cocoa powder
>
> Pinch of salt
>
> ³/₄   cup heavy cream
>
> 1   teaspoon vanilla extract

In a medium saucepan, melt the butter. Stir in the sugar, cocoa, and salt. Gradually stir in the cream. Heat, stirring constantly, until the mixture is smooth and hot but not boiling. Remove from the heat and stir in the vanilla. Cool until thickened to the consistency of frosting, or use warm for a glaze or sauce. *Store leftover frosting in the refrigerator. Rewarm gently in a pan of barely simmering water or in a microwave before using.*

farmhouse chocolate cake

from ONE POTATO TWO POTATO

makes one 10-inch tube cake | This is a rich, moist cake, the kind of cake that you'd find on a big scrubbed pine table. It cries out for a glass of cold milk.

Pepper's controversial. Some folks just can't imagine why you'd add it to a cake, but we think it gives a great zing. You can skip it if it scares you.

desserts

$3/4$ pound all-purpose potatoes, peeled and cut into chunks

Coarse salt

Cocoa powder for dusting

5   ounces unsweetened chocolate, chopped

2   tablespoons honey

$1/2$ cup boiling water

$1 3/4$ cups all-purpose flour

2   teaspoons baking soda

$1/4$–$1/2$ teaspoon freshly ground black pepper

8   tablespoons (1 stick) unsalted butter, at room temperature

$1/4$ cup vegetable shortening

2   cups sugar

5   large eggs, at room temperature

2   teaspoons vanilla extract

Confectioners' sugar for dusting (optional)

Put the potatoes in a saucepan, cover with cold water by at least an inch, add a pinch of salt, and bring to a boil. Cook until the potatoes are tender. Drain well, put the potatoes through a ricer, and measure out 1 cup.

Heat the oven to 350 degrees. Butter a 10-inch tube pan and dust it generously with cocoa.

Put the chocolate and honey in a small bowl. Pour in the boiling water and leave the chocolate to melt and cool, stirring occasionally until it's very smooth.

▼

FOOD & WINE test-kitchen tips

- If you'd like to dress up this cake, try serving it with brown-sugar whipped cream. Just add 2 table-spoons dark brown sugar to 1 cup heavy cream and beat.

- The cake is so moist that it keeps very well for 3 days.

Sift the flour, baking soda, a pinch of salt, and the pepper together.

Cut the butter into chunks and put it in a large mixing bowl. Beat with an electric mixer until light. Add the vegetable shortening and beat until combined and light. Gradually pour in the sugar and beat until this mixture is very light and fluffy. Add the eggs one by one, beating for at least a minute after each addition. Beat in the chocolate, then the potatoes, then the vanilla. Scrape the sides of the bowl.

Add the dry ingredients to the batter alternately with $\frac{1}{2}$ cup cold water, stirring just until combined and smooth.

Scrape the batter into the pan, shake the pan and rap it lightly on the counter to get rid of any air bubbles, and bake until the cake tests done (a skewer will come out clean), about 50 minutes. Cool in the pan on a rack for 10 minutes or so, then turn out the cake, flip it right side up, and leave it on a rack to cool completely.

If you want, dust the cake generously with confectioners' sugar right before serving.

desserts

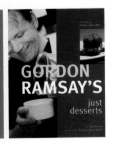

dark and delicious chocolate torte

from GORDON RAMSAY'S JUST DESSERTS

serves 6–8 | It seems every chef must have his or her ultimate orgiastic chocolate recipe, with names like chocolate decadence, indulgence, or nemesis. Well, this is mine. It is based on the little, hot chocolate fondants we serve in the winter—it occurred to me that if I left out the flour and cocoa powder, I could bake the mixture as a whole torte to be eaten cool. You will find that the top bakes to a slight crispness, which when the torte is unmolded becomes a light, crunchy base.

to coat the pan
Scant 2 tbsp. (25 g) butter, melted
1 oz. (25 g) bittersweet chocolate, grated

torte
12 oz. (350 g) good-quality bittersweet chocolate
1 tbsp. instant coffee
2 tbsp. boiling water
2–3 tbsp. brandy
4 extra large eggs, separated
7 tbsp. (100 g) unsalted butter, softened
$1/8$ tsp. salt
1 cup (200 g) superfine sugar

1 To prepare the cake pan, cut a disk of baking parchment to fit the bottom of an 8 in. (20 cm) springform cake pan or a moule à manquer mold; set the paper aside. Brush the inside of the pan or mold with the melted butter and chill until set. Then coat the side with the grated chocolate, tapping out any excess. Fit the disk of baking parchment on the bottom. Set aside.

FOOD & WINE test-kitchen tips

- Bittersweet and semisweet chocolate are the same thing, although good-quality chocolate is more often labeled bittersweet.

- A *moule à manquer* is a French cake pan that has slightly sloping sides that are about $1^{1}/2$ inches high. You can use an American cake pan for this dessert, just as long as it's fairly deep. The sloping sides aren't necessary.

2 For the torte, break up the chocolate and place in a large, heatproof bowl. Dissolve the coffee in the boiling water, then stir in the brandy and pour over the chocolate. Microwave for about 2 minutes on High, or set the bowl over a pan of gently simmering water until the chocolate has melted. Stir until smooth, then let cool. Preheat the oven to 350°F.

3 Beat the egg yolks and butter together in a bowl until creamy, then beat in the cooled chocolate mixture.

4 In another bowl, beat the egg whites with the salt until softly stiff, then gradually beat in the sugar until you have a firm, glossy meringue.

5 Carefully fold the meringue into the chocolate mixture, one-third at a time, until it is evenly incorporated. Spoon the batter into the prepared cake pan or mold and gently level the surface. Bake the cake for about 40 minutes until risen and the top is crisp. The surface might crack a little, which is fine, and the mixture underneath will still be soft. That is as it should be.

6 Turn off the oven and leave the cake to cool inside for about an hour. Then remove and let cool completely. Do not chill—this torte should be moist and soft.

7 To unmold, run a table knife around the side of the torte to loosen it, then invert onto a serving plate. Lift off the side of the pan and the base. Cut the torte into wedges using a knife dipped into hot water.

serve with a pitcher of cream, or with sour cream or creme fraiche

caramelized coconut budino from JOANNE WEIR'S

MORE COOKING IN THE WINE COUNTRY

serves 8 | I've never really liked coconut, but when a Tuscan friend of mine served this dish recently, I changed my mind. I'd been invited to breakfast and expected the usual breakfast fare. Instead she served two desserts, including this *budino*, or custard, that magically separates itself into three layers.

2^1/$_2$ cups very finely grated sweetened coconut

2 cups sugar

8 eggs

3 cups whole milk

3 tablespoons all-purpose flour

Preheat the oven to 325°F.

Place the coconut on a baking sheet and bake in the oven until light golden, tossing occasionally, 10 to 12 minutes. Let cool slightly. Place in a food processor and pulse until finely ground. Reserve. Increase oven temperature to 375°F.

In a large, heavy stainless-steel frying pan, melt 1 cup of the sugar over medium heat. Do not stir with a spoon; instead, swirl the pan to melt the sugar uniformly. Cook until the sugar starts to turn golden brown. Immediately remove the pan from the heat and pour the mixture into an 8-inch cake pan. Turn the cake pan to coat the bottom and sides with caramel. Set it aside.

Whisk the eggs together in a bowl. Add the remaining 1 cup sugar, the milk, coconut, and flour, and stir together until well mixed.

FOOD & WINE test-kitchen tips

- The author suggests serving this custard tart hot out of the oven. It's good cold too. In fact, we thought it was even better after several hours in the refrigerator.

- A water bath, such as the one used here, keeps custard from getting too hot and curdling. If your cake pan is shallow, you may need to use less hot water than suggested. Pour in enough to come about halfway up the side of the pan.

Pour the coconut mixture into the caramel-lined pan, and place in a larger pan. Pour boiling water into the larger pan to a depth of one inch. Bake in the oven until set and a skewer goes into the center and comes out clean, 55 to 65 minutes.

Remove the cake pan from the larger pan and let it sit for 10 minutes. Then invert the coconut *budino* onto a serving plate, and serve.

blueberry brown butter tart from JOANNE WEIR'S

MORE COOKING IN THE WINE COUNTRY

serves 8 | Blueberries crown this beautiful and great-tasting tart. Brown butter is called *beurre noisette*, "hazelnut butter," in French. The butter is cooked until it turns a light hazelnut brown and imparts a nutty aroma. The flavor marries particularly well with fruit—blueberries as well as other varieties.

3	eggs
1¼	cups sugar
1	tablespoon grated lemon zest
1	teaspoon vanilla extract
¼	cup all-purpose flour, sifted
12	tablespoons (1½ sticks) unsalted butter
1	prebaked Sweet Short Crust Tart Shell (page 240)
1	cup fresh blueberries

topping

2	cups water
1½	cups sugar
2½	cups fresh blueberries
½	cup confectioners' sugar

In a large bowl, whisk the eggs, sugar, lemon zest, and vanilla extract until combined. Sift the flour over the top and mix well. Set aside.

In a small saucepan over medium-high heat, melt the butter until it is foamy. Continue to heat the butter until the foam begins to subside and the butter begins to turn brown, just starts to smoke, and gives off a nutty aroma. Whisking continuously, pour the hot butter in a steady stream into the egg mixture, combining well. Let the mixture cool to room temperature.

▼

FOOD & WINE test-kitchen tips

- For a tablespoon of grated lemon zest, you'll need 2 to 3 lemons.

- Out-of-season blueberries are okay in this recipe; in fact, their tartness contrasts nicely with the sweetness of the filling.

- A fluted pan with a removable bottom makes an especially attractive tart that's easy to unmold. If you don't have a tart pan, though, you'll get the same delicious dessert using a pie plate.

Preheat the oven to 350°F.

Sprinkle the 1 cup blueberries evenly over the bottom of the prebaked tart shell. Pour the brown butter mixture over the blueberries, filling the shell two-thirds full. Bake until the filling is firm to the touch, 45 to 55 minutes. Let the tart cool completely.

For the topping, combine the water and sugar in a saucepan, and bring to a boil over medium heat. Boil for 30 seconds. Place the blueberries in a colander set over a bowl. Pour the syrup over the berries, coating them completely and allowing the excess to run into the bowl. Shake the colander to remove the excess syrup. Mound the berries onto the cooled tart, covering the entire top.

Just before serving, sift the confectioners' sugar over the top.

sweet short crust tart shell | makes one 9-inch tart shell

1¼ cups all-purpose flour

1   tablespoon sugar

Pinch of salt

1   teaspoon grated lemon zest

10   tablespoons (1¼ sticks) unsalted butter, out of the refrigerator
     for 15 minutes, cut into small pieces

Up to 1 tablespoon water, room temperature

In a food processor, mix the flour, sugar, and salt with a few pulses. Add the lemon zest and butter, and pulse until the mixture resembles cornmeal. Add the water as needed until the dough just holds together in a ball. Remove the dough from the processor and flatten it into a 6-inch-diameter cake. Wrap it in plastic wrap and refrigerate for 30 minutes.

Preheat the oven to 400°F.

Press the pastry evenly onto the bottom and sides of a 9-inch tart pan. Chill the tart shell in the freezer for 30 minutes.

Line the pastry with baking parchment, and scatter 1 cup of dried beans or pie weights onto the parchment. Bake the tart shell until the top edges are light golden, 10 to 15 minutes. Remove the parchment and weights, reduce the heat to 375°F, and continue to bake until the shell is light golden, 15 to 20 minutes.

a pair of apple dumplings baked in cinnamon sauce

from FEARLESS BAKING

serves 2 | Need something warm to soothe you on a cold winter evening? Forget the soup. Sit down in front of a crackling fire with one of these warm apple dumplings, and you'll forget all about the cold temperatures outside. Whole peeled apples are wrapped in piecrust and basted during the baking with a cinnamon sauce that forms a brittle, candy-like coating wherever it coats the crust. It's the perfect ending to a cozy dinner for two.

baking answers Apples are peeled and cored but left whole for apple dumplings. An apple corer is the best tool for coring a whole apple, but a small paring knife will do the job. Use the knife to cut a cone out of the center of the apple, cutting out the stem and cutting the cone as deeply as you can. Turn the apple over and cut a cone from the bottom. Stand the apple stem end up and work the knife around the hole in the center to make a hole through the center of the apple that removes the core and any seeds.

Cool the cinnamon sauce slightly before pouring it over the apples. Hot cinnamon sauce can melt the butter in the dough and soften the dough before it bakes and sets.

a step ahead Mix the piecrust dough 1 day ahead, cover with plastic wrap, and refrigerate. The dumplings can be assembled and put in their pan, but without the sauce, 4 to 5 hours ahead of time. Cover with plastic wrap and refrigerate until ready to pour over the sauce and bake them.

You can bake the dumplings a day ahead, then warm them before serving them.

necessities One 9-inch-diameter shiny metal or glass pie pan or 2 individual oval or round shallow-sided ovenproof dishes about 6 inches across (such as au gratin dishes), a rolling pin, and one 1-crust recipe cold Fearless Piecrust dough (page 244)

FOOD & WINE test-kitchen tips

- These dumplings also taste superb baked in nutmeg, cardamom, or ginger sauce. Just use the same quantity of the chosen spice instead of cinnamon in both the sauce and the apple filling.

- The recipe suggests serving the dumplings with fresh cream, a fine thing indeed—but wait until you try them with vanilla ice cream.

cinnamon sauce

$1/2$ cup water

$1/4$ cup sugar

$1/2$ teaspoon ground cinnamon

1   tablespoon unsalted butter

1   recipe cold Fearless Piecrust dough (page 244)

apple filling

2   medium apples, peeled, cored, and left whole

2   teaspoons unsalted butter

2   teaspoons sugar

$1/8$ teaspoon ground cinnamon

cook the sauce

Position a rack in the middle of the oven. Preheat the oven to 400°F. Butter a 9-inch pie pan or 2 individual baking dishes with shallow sides about 1 inch high and about 6 inches across at the widest point.

Put the water, sugar, cinnamon, and butter in a small saucepan and cook over medium heat, stirring often, until the sugar dissolves and the butter melts. Set the sauce aside to cool while you prepare the dumplings.

make the dumplings

Lightly flour the rolling surface and rolling pin. Roll the piecrust dough into a long rectangle 17 x 8½ inches. Trim the edges and cut two 8-inch squares. Use a thin metal spatula to loosen the dough from the rolling surface and transfer each square to the baking pan. Cut a thin slice off the bottom of each apple so the bottom is flat. Put 1 apple in the center of each square of dough. Then, press 1 teaspoon of butter into the center of one of the apples and sprinkle with half of the sugar and cinnamon. Bring up the corners of the square to the top center of the apple and seal. Pinch the seams to seal them well, but don't press them flat against the apple. Leave them poking out so they look like 4 segments of thin wings coming out from the apple. If thick seams form, trim them slightly with a small knife. Check for any breaks in the dough and press dough scraps onto any breaks to repair them. Repeat with the second piece of dough and apple, placing the dumplings at least 1 inch apart. Use a fork to prick the pastry twice on the top of each dumpling. You can cut out 4 oval leaf shapes from scraps of dough and press 2 each onto the top of each dumpling for decoration. Pour all of the cinnamon sauce over the apples. It will be thin and run off the dumplings.

bake the dumplings

Bake 35 minutes, until the crust is light brown. The edges of the seams turn slightly darker. Use a large spoon to baste the dumplings with the sauce after the first 15 minutes of baking and again after an additional 10 minutes of baking. The dumplings will have baked for 25 minutes before the second basting and the sauce will be thick and syrupy and cling to the crust. Spoon as much sauce as possible over the dumplings during this second basting. The baked dumplings are glazed over much of the crust with a crisp, shiny layer of cinnamon sauce.

serve the dumplings

If the dumplings are baked in a pie pan, immediately use a wide flat spatula to carefully transfer each dumpling to a shallow bowl or dish. Transfer them before the glaze sets so they don't stick to the pan. If baked in individual dishes, serve the dumplings in their baking dishes. Cool slightly for about 10 minutes. Serve warm with fresh cream to pour over, if desired. If the crust should split slightly while the dumplings bake (which seldom happens), press the crust edges together gently. The sticky glaze holds the crust together. However, a small split in the crust gives the dumpling an appealing, homey look. The dumplings can be baked a day ahead and left in their baking pan to be cooled, covered, and stored at room temperature. Uncover the dumplings and warm them in a preheated 275°F. oven for 20 minutes. Warming the dumplings releases the bottoms from the baking pan again.

fearless piecrust | **makes 1 or 2 piecrusts for a 9-inch pie pan** | Since my mother was not comfortable making piecrusts, it followed in my mind that if my great-baker mom couldn't make piecrust, it must be hard. I was over thirty when I attempted my first crust. It was too bad that I waited so long, because a flaky, buttery, homemade piecrust has no equal, and it isn't hard after all, but rather a matter of paying attention to a few guidelines. As long as I kept the shortening cold, mixed the shortening into the flour quickly to produce a flour-coated crumbly mixture, and added as little cold water as possible to form the soft dough, I was rolling out pie dough with ease. Even my mom was impressed.

When I set out to develop this piecrust recipe, I wanted anyone to feel comfortable making it. At the same time I was asked to edit some recipes for the Culinary Institute of America in Hyde Park, New York. Their piecrust recipe had a clever technique that worked so well I adapted it from then on for all of my piecrusts. The butter and vegetable shortening are softened and blended to a smooth mass, then frozen for at least 5 hours. The frozen shortening is coarsely grated and then immediately stirred into the flour. The frozen shortening can even be grated in a food processor. The small grated pieces produce the desired crumbly shortening-and-flour mixture effortlessly. The final step is to stir in enough cold water to form a dough. This is a yes-you-can piecrust that I hope you'll try.

Please don't be put off by the length of these directions. The pie dough actually takes minutes to prepare and roll, but I wanted to pass on what I've learned so you would feel confident making piecrust.

baking answers This piecrust includes butter for flavor and vegetable shortening for flakiness. A combination of all-purpose and cake flour for the flour lowers the gluten content of the total flour and ensures a more tender crust. It's like a little safety net to make the crust tender. The butter and shortening mixture must be frozen and should be added to the flour as soon as it's grated. Grate the shortening on the large holes of a grater, holding the frozen piece of shortening with a clean dish towel or several layers of aluminum foil so the warmth of your hand doesn't warm it. Even better, grate the shortening in a food processor fitted with the grating blade.

Pie dough often requires slightly less liquid on a warm, humid day and slightly more liquid on a cold, dry day. The same brand of flour may use more liquid at different times of the year. This is why recipes for piecrust often give a flexible measurement that usually varies by 1 to 2 teaspoons for the amount of liquid that is used.

Cold tiny pieces of shortening form little fat pockets in the crust that make a crust with flaky layers. You'll actually be able to see the layers in a piece of baked crust. Use ice water for the liquid to avoid warming the shortening. Once the dough is mixed you can gather it into a ball without worrying. It would take a lot of handling with warm hands to toughen the dough. The dough rests in the refrigerator to relax the gluten in the flour that has become stretched by the mixing process. Once chilled, the cold dough rolls out easily and doesn't stick to the rolling surface. A clean kitchen counter works well for rolling dough.

▼

245

One of the problems people have mentioned that they have with piecrust is that it becomes hard after it bakes. This happens when the fat is not mixed enough with the flour to form small crumbs, which requires additional liquid to be added to form a dough. As you know from playing with it as a child, flour and water make paste, so a dough that has too much water bakes into a firm pastelike crust. My method of grating the frozen shortening makes it so easy to blend the fat and flour that it virtually eliminates this possible problem.

I use Crisco for the vegetable shortening. Try to buy the easy-to-measure sticks of vegetable shortening rather than the cans of shortening. Do not use butter-flavor Crisco.

In the unlikely event that the piecrust tears or cracks when you transfer it to the pie pan, press scraps of dough onto any holes to seal them.

a step ahead Disks of piecrust dough can be covered and refrigerated overnight and rolled out the next day. The dough will need to soften until it rolls out easily. Or pie pans can be lined with the rolled piecrust, covered, and refrigerated overnight.

Unbaked piecrust can be rolled, pressed into its pan, wrapped tightly, and frozen for up to 1 month. Frozen piecrust in a metal pan does not need to defrost before baking but will take about 5 minutes longer to bake than cold, defrosted piecrust. The unrolled disks of dough can also be wrapped with plastic wrap and foil and frozen for up to 1 month. Defrost the wrapped frozen dough overnight in the refrigerator and let it soften at room temperature just until it is soft enough to roll out easily. I defrost piecrusts that are frozen in ovenproof glass pans in the refrigerator to avoid the possibility of the frozen pie dish breaking when it is put in a hot oven. With a piecrust ready to go in the freezer, many pie fillings can be mixed so quickly that the pies can be ready to bake in about 10 minutes.

necessities One 9-inch pie pan, a grater for the frozen shortening mixture (which freezes for at least 5 hours), and a rolling pin

for 1 piecrust

5   tablespoons soft unsalted butter

4   tablespoons ($1/4$ cup) soft vegetable shortening

1   cup unbleached all-purpose flour

$1/3$ cup cake flour

1   tablespoon sugar

$1/4$ teaspoon salt

3   tablespoons plus 2 to 3 teaspoons ice water

for 2 piecrusts or a 2-crusted pie

10   tablespoons ($1 1/4$ sticks) soft unsalted butter

8   tablespoons ($1/2$ cup) soft vegetable shortening

2   cups unbleached all-purpose flour

$2/3$ cup cake flour

2   tablespoons sugar

$1/2$ teaspoon salt

7 to 8 tablespoons ice water

mix the dough

Butter a 9-inch-diameter metal or glass pie pan.

Put the butter and vegetable shortening in a medium bowl and beat with an electric mixer on medium speed until they are blended smoothly together, about 1 minute. Scrape the mixture onto a piece of plastic wrap and form it into a rectangle about 4 x $2 1/2$ inches and about 1 inch thick. This shape is easy to hold for grating and can fit or be cut to fit in the feed tube of a food processor. Wrap in the plastic wrap and freeze firm, at least 5 hours or overnight. If making 2 piecrusts, form the shortening into 2 rectangles for easier grating.

Put both flours, sugar, and salt in a large bowl and stir to combine the ingredients. Set aside.

▼

Remove 1 piece of frozen shortening (if there are 2 pieces) from the freezer and unwrap it. Holding the shortening with a clean dish towel to prevent warm hands from melting it and using the large holes of a grater, grate the shortening onto a piece of wax paper. If there is a little piece left at the end, cut it into tiny pieces to add to the flour. Grate the second frozen piece, if making 2 crusts. Or, grate the frozen shortening in a food processor fitted with the grating blade. Immediately add the grated shortening to the flour mixture. Use a fork to stir the shortening into the flour until it is completely blended and looks crumbly, about 40 strokes. Or, use an electric mixer to mix the shortening and flour for about 15 seconds until it forms crumbs. The largest crumbs will be about ¼ inch in size. Sprinkle 3 tablespoons of ice water (or 7 tablespoons of ice water for 2 piecrusts) over the mixture, stirring it with the fork or electric mixer. Add additional water by teaspoonfuls, stirring it in just until there is no loose flour and a dough forms that holds together in clumps. The dough should feel cold.

Gather the dough together and turn it out onto a lightly floured rolling surface. With the heel of your hand push the dough down and forward against the rolling surface 3 or 4 times to form a smooth dough (6 or 7 times for 2 piecrusts). A couple of additional strokes with the heel of your hand in order to form a smooth dough is fine. Gather the dough into a ball, then press it into a disk about 5 inches in diameter (2 disks if making 2 piecrusts). The dough feels soft and malleable, but not sticky. The dough is easier to roll into a circle if it is round and the edges are smooth, but don't handle it a lot just to get smooth edges or a perfect circle. Wrap the dough in plastic wrap and chill it in the refrigerator for at least 30 minutes or as long as overnight.

At this point the dough can be wrapped in plastic wrap and heavy aluminum foil, labeled with the date and contents, and frozen for up to 1 month.

chocolate banana blintzes

from **A YEAR IN CHOCOLATE** | serves 6 (3 blintzes each)

This is a great party dessert. The blintzes look complicated (which they aren't) and fancy (which they are). Simple do-ahead steps can be completed a day or more in advance. A few minutes of your attention at serving time are amply rewarded when the first fork breaks a tender crepe bursting with bananas and warm chocolate sauce.

ingredients

crepes

3   eggs

1   cup all-purpose flour

$^1/_8$ teaspoon salt

$1^3/_4$ cups milk

2   tablespoons melted butter

Butter or oil, for frying

sauce

7   ounces bittersweet or semisweet chocolate, chopped into small pieces

$^1/_2$ cup milk

2   teaspoons sugar

$^1/_2$ teaspoon vanilla extract

3   large ripe bananas

Butter, for frying

Sour cream, for serving

equipment

6-inch frying pan

Tray, lined with wax paper

To make crepes, combine eggs, flour, salt, milk, and melted butter in a blender or food processor. Pulse just until blended. Chill for 1 hour or up to 1 day.

▼

FOOD & WINE test-kitchen tips

- The crepes in this recipe are especially easy to make because they're sautéed on only one side. Fill with the browned side down so that it will be on the outside when the blintz is formed.

- The last sentence of the recipe is "Serve plain or with sour cream." There's no question in our minds about which way to go. The sour cream is too perfect with the bananas and chocolate to skip it.

Heat a 6-inch frying pan over medium-high heat. Brush the pan lightly with butter. Pour 2 table-spoons of batter into the pan and tilt the pan immediately to coat the entire surface evenly. Cook until the crepe is uniformly translucent and the surface no longer looks wet, 45 seconds to 1 minute. Loosen the crepe's edges with a spatula and invert the pan over a piece of wax paper. If necessary, unfold the fallen crepe, but try not to make holes in it. Repeat with the remaining batter, buttering the pan when necessary. *Use the crepes immediately, or stack between sheets of wax paper, covered airtight, and refrigerate up to 2 days.*

To make the sauce, mix chocolate, milk, and sugar in the top of a double boiler over barely simmering water. Or microwave on Medium (50 percent) power, about 2 minutes. Stir frequently until smooth. Remove from heat and stir in vanilla. Use the warm sauce immediately or set aside and use cool. *The sauce keeps several days in the refrigerator. Rewarm gently before use.*

To assemble the blintzes, slice the bananas ¼ inch thick. Place 3 banana slices in a row, hor-izontally, in the middle of a crepe. Spread 1 tablespoon of sauce over the slices. Fold the 2 sides of the crepe over the bananas. Fold the top of the crepe down over the bananas. Fold the bottom up to overlap. Carefully place each blintz on a tray. Repeat to assemble all of the blintzes. Cover tightly with plastic wrap. Refrigerate the blintzes at least 1 hour or up to 2 days.

To serve, heat a large frying pan over medium-high heat. When the pan is hot, add 1 table-spoon of butter and swirl to coat the pan. Add as many blintzes to the pan as will fit comfort-ably. Cook until just browned, about 30 seconds. Turn the blintzes carefully and brown the bot-toms. Place the blintzes on a warm serving plate. Serve plain or with sour cream.

orange curd layer pudding

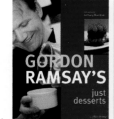

from GORDON RAMSAY'S JUST DESSERTS

serves 4–6 | This delightful, old-fashioned pudding cooks to a delicious light soufflé sponge on top, with a thick, zingy curd sauce underneath. It looks like a nightmare just before you bake it, all runny and slightly lumpy—the transformation is little short of a miracle. I wonder whoever first thought of such a recipe, or was it a happy accident? Bake it in a heatproof glass dish to reveal the appealing layers. For a dinner party, add a splash of Grand Marnier or Cointreau.

1¼ cups (300 ml) fresh orange juice

Grated zest and juice of 1 lemon

3   tbsp. Grand Marnier or Cointreau (optional)

4   tbsp. (60 g) butter, softened, plus extra for greasing the dish

½   cup (100 g) granulated sugar

4   extra large eggs, separated

7   tbsp. (60 g) self-rising flour

½   tsp. baking powder

⅔   cup (150 ml) milk

Confectioners' sugar, for sprinkling

1 Put the orange and lemon juices in a saucepan, bring to a boil, and boil until reduced by half. Let cool, then stir in the liqueur, if using.

2 Butter the sides of a 1 quart (1 liter) glass soufflé dish, or other similar baking dish. Preheat the oven to 350°F.

3 In a mixing bowl, beat the butter with the sugar and lemon zest until soft and creamy. Beat in the egg yolks, one at a time. Sift the flour and baking powder together over the mixture, then beat in.

▼

FOOD & WINE test-kitchen tips

- If self-rising flour isn't available in your area, you can make it by adding ¾ teaspoon baking powder and ¼ teaspoon salt per ½ cup of flour.

- You can make this appealing dessert in other flavors too. For instance, you might substitute lemon or lime juice for the orange juice, omit the Grand Marnier, and double the sugar.

4 Slowly add the orange juice and milk to the mixture, stirring to blend. Do not worry if the mixture looks curdled or lumpy at this stage. It will be fine. Trust me—I'm a chef.

5 Beat the egg whites in another bowl until they will form softly stiff peaks. Beat one-third of the egg whites into the orange mixture, then carefully fold in the remaining whites, using a large metal spoon and a figure-of-eight motion.

6 Set the prepared dish in a roasting pan, then pour in the pudding mixture. Add boiling water to the roasting pan, to surround the dish, and place in the oven. Bake for 1–1¼ hours until the pudding is golden brown and firm on top; it will be creamy underneath. Reduce the oven temperature slightly toward the end of cooking if the top seems to be browning too quickly.

7 Remove the dish from the pan of water and let stand for 10 minutes or so. Dust the pudding with confectioners' sugar before serving. As you spoon it out, make sure you get right down to the bottom, to include some of the soft curd layer with each spoonful.

pecan sticky buns from NUTS

yields 18 buns | The real thing: old-fashioned extra-gooey sticky buns, baked upside down and then flipped out of the pan to reveal a topping of pecans with a cinnamon-caramel glaze.

1$\frac{1}{4}$ cups warm milk (110° to 115°)

$\frac{1}{4}$ cup warm water (110° to 115°)

6$\frac{3}{4}$ teaspoons ($\frac{3}{4}$ ounce) active dry yeast

$\frac{1}{2}$ cup granulated sugar

1 tablespoon vanilla extract

2 teaspoons salt

$\frac{1}{2}$ cup unsalted butter, cut into pieces, at room temperature

2 eggs

5 to 5$\frac{1}{2}$ cups flour

glaze

3 cups pecans

3 cups packed dark brown sugar

1 cup unsalted butter

$\frac{1}{2}$ cup light corn syrup

1$\frac{1}{2}$ teaspoons ground cinnamon

2 teaspoons vanilla extract

In a large bowl, combine milk, water, and yeast. Stir to blend. Let stand until yeast is foamy, 5 to 10 minutes. Stir in granulated sugar, vanilla, and salt. Whisk in butter pieces and eggs until eggs are well blended (any remaining lumps of butter will disappear with further mixing).

Beat in 2$\frac{1}{2}$ cups of the flour. Beat in enough of the remaining flour, about 2$\frac{1}{2}$ cups, to make a manageable dough that holds together in a rough mass. Turn out onto a floured work surface and knead 2 minutes. Let dough rest 10 minutes. Resume kneading, adding more flour if dough is sticky, until dough is smooth and elastic. Place in an oiled bowl, cover with a towel, and let rise in a draft-free place until dough is doubled in bulk, about 1 hour.

FOOD & WINE test-kitchen tips

- As the recipe states, these luscious sticky buns should be served warm—not finger-burning hot. After removing them from the pan, let them sit for 10 minutes before you dive in.

- If you don't want so much temptation around the house, you can cut this recipe in half with no problems.

Meanwhile, make the glaze: Preheat oven to 350°. Spread pecans on a baking sheet or in a shallow pan. Bake, stirring once or twice, until lightly browned and fragrant, 7 to 10 minutes. Let cool slightly, then chop coarsely.

In a large saucepan, combine brown sugar, butter, corn syrup, and cinnamon. Cook over medium heat, stirring, until mixture is smooth and bubbles begin to appear around edges of pan. Stir in vanilla.

Butter two 8-inch-square baking pans. Spread 1 cup glaze in each pan; top each with 1 cup toasted pecans. Stir the remaining cup pecans into glaze in saucepan. Set aside.

Punch down dough. Turn onto a lightly floured work surface; divide into 2 equal portions. Roll or pat 1 portion into a 9- by 14-inch rectangle. Spread dough with half the remaining glaze. Roll up jelly-roll fashion, beginning with the long edge; pinch seam to seal. With a serrated knife, gently cut roll into 9 slices, each about 1½ inches thick. Place slices, cut side down, in one of the prepared pans. Repeat with remaining dough and glaze.

Let rise, uncovered, until dough is not quite doubled, 40 to 60 minutes.

Preheat oven to 375°. Place a foil-covered baking sheet on a rack just beneath the sticky buns to catch any glaze that might drip. Bake until buns are puffed and golden and glaze is hot and bubbly, 40 to 50 minutes. Let cool in pan up to 5 minutes. Invert each pan onto a large, heat-proof serving platter; wait a few seconds, then carefully lift off hot pans. Serve warm.

recipes by book

▼

recipes by book

▼

credits & acknowledgments

Artisan
(a division of Workman Publishing, Inc.)
708 Broadway
New York, NY 10003
(212) 254-5900
www.workman.com

- **A New Way to Cook** by Sally Schneider. Copyright © 2001 by Sally Schneider. Reprinted by permission of Sally Schneider and Artisan, a division of Workman Publishing, Inc. Photographs copyright © by Maria Robledo.

Bloomsbury Publishing
175 Fifth Avenue
New York, NY 10010
(212) 674-5151
www.bloomsbury.com

- **Da Silvano Cookbook** *Simple Secrets from New York's Favorite Italian Restaurant* by Silvano Marchetto. Copyright © 2001 by Silvano Marchetto. Reprinted by permission of Bloomsbury Publishing. Photographs by Robert DiScalfani.

Chronicle Books
85 Second Street
San Francisco, CA 94105
(415) 537-3730
www.chroniclebooks.com

- **Enoteca** *Simple, Delicious Recipes in the Italian Wine Bar Tradition* by Joyce Goldstein with wine notes by Evan Goldstein. Text copyright © 2001 by Joyce Goldstein. Reprinted by permission of Chronicle Books. Photographs copyright © 2001 by Angela Wyant.

▼

Clarkson Potter/Publishers
(member of the Crown Publishing Group)
Random House, Inc.
1540 Broadway
New York, NY 10036
(212) 782-9000
www.randomhouse.com

■ **La Bella Cucina** *How to Cook, Eat, and Live Like an Italian* by Viana La Place. Copyright © 2001 by Viana La Place. Reprinted by permission of Random House, Inc.

The Ecco Press
(a division of HarperCollins Publishers Inc.)
10 East 53rd Street
New York, NY 10022
(212) 207-7000
www.harpercollins.com

■ **Madhur Jaffrey's Step-by-Step Cooking** *Over 150 Dishes from India and the Far East, Including Thailand, Vietnam, Indonesia, and Malaysia* by Madhur Jaffrey. Text copyright © 2001 by Madhur Jaffrey. Reprinted by permission of HarperCollins Publishers Inc. Photographs copyright © 2001 by Gus Fligate and Craig Robertson.

HarperCollins Publishers
10 East 53rd Street
New York, NY 10022
(212) 207-7000
www.harpercollins.com

■ **Second Helpings from Union Square Cafe** *140 New Favorites from New York's Acclaimed Restaurant* by Danny Meyer and Michael Romano. Copyright © 2001 by Danny Meyer and Michael Romano. Reprinted by permission of HarperCollins Publishers Inc. Photographs by Duane Michals.

■ **Pleasures of the Vietnamese Table** *Recipes and Reminiscences from Vietnam's Best Market Kitchens, Street Cafés, and Home Cooks* by Mai Pham. Copyright © 2001 by Mai Pham. Reprinted by permission of HarperCollins Publishers Inc. Photographs by Mai Pham.

Houghton Mifflin Company
215 Park Avenue South
New York, NY 10003
(212) 420-5800
www.hmco.com

■ **One Potato, Two Potato** *300 Recipes from Simple to Elegant—Appetizers, Main Dishes, Side Dishes, and More* by Roy Finamore with Molly Stevens. Copyright © 2001 by Roy Finamore. Reprinted by permission of Houghton Mifflin Company. Photographs copyright © 2001 by Kelly Bugden.

Hyperion
77 West 66th Street
New York, NY 10023
(800) 759-0190
www.hyperionbooks.com

■ **The Naked Chef Takes Off** by Jamie Oliver. Copyright © 2000 by Jamie Oliver Ltd. Reprinted by permission of Hyperion. Photographs copyright © 2001 by David Loftus.

■ **Bobby Flay Cooks American** *Great Regional Recipes with Sizzling New Flavors* by Bobby Flay with Julia Moskin. Copyright © 2001 by Bobby Flay. Reprinted by permission of Hyperion. Photographs copyright © 2001 by Gentl & Hyers/Edge.

▼

Laurel Glen Publishing

(an imprint of the Advantage Publishers Group)

5880 Oberlin Drive

San Diego, CA 92121

(858) 457-2500

www.advantagebooksonline.com

- **Gordon Ramsay's Just Desserts** by Gordon Ramsay with Roz Denny. Text copyright © by Gordon Ramsay. Reprinted by permission of Laurel Glen, an imprint of the Advantage Publishers Group. Photographs copyright © by Georgia Glynn Smith.

Little, Brown and Company

(an AOL Time Warner company)

1271 Avenue of the Americas

New York, NY 10020

(212) 522-8700

www.twbookmark.com

- **The Elements of Taste** by Gray Kunz and Peter Kaminsky. Copyright © 2001 by Gray Kunz and Peter Kaminsky. Reprinted by permission of Little, Brown and Company. Photographs by André Baranowski.

William Morrow and Company

(an imprint of HarperCollins Publishers Inc.)

10 East 53rd Street

New York, NY 10022

(212) 207-7000

www.harpercollins.com

- **Biba's Taste of Italy** *Recipes from the Homes, Trattorie, and Restaurants of Emilia-Romagna* by Biba Caggiano. Copyright © 2001 by Biba Caggiano. Reprinted by permission of HarperCollins Publishers Inc. Photographs by Stuart Schwartz.

- **Prime Time Emeril** *More TV Dinners from America's Favorite Chef* by Emeril Lagasse. Copyright © 2001 by Emeril's Food of Love Productions LLC. Reprinted by permission of HarperCollins Publishers Inc. Photographs by Quentin Bacon.

- **The Baker's Dozen Cookbook** *Become a Better Baker with 135 Foolproof Recipes and Tried-and-True Techniques* edited by Rick Rodgers. Copyright © 2001 by the Baker's Dozen, Inc., a California not-for-profit corporation. Reprinted by permission of HarperCollins Publishers Inc. Photographs by Beatriz Da Costa.

- **Italian Holiday Cooking** *A Collection of 150 Treasured Recipes* by Michele Scicolone. Copyright © 2001 by Michele Scicolone. Reprinted by permission of HarperCollins Publishers Inc. Photographs by Ellen Silverman.

Scribner
(a division of Simon & Schuster)
1230 Avenue of the Americas
New York, NY 10020
(212) 698-7000
www.simonsays.com

- **Joanne Weir's More Cooking in the Wine Country** by Joanne Weir. Text copyright © 2001 by Joanne Weir. Reprinted by permission of Simon & Schuster. Photographs copyright © 2001 by Penina.

Simon & Schuster
1230 Avenue of the Americas
New York, NY 10020
(212) 698-7000
www.simonsays.com

- **Fearless Baking** *Over 100 Recipes That Anyone Can Make* by Elinor Klivans. Copyright © 2001 by Elinor Klivans. Reprinted by permission of Simon & Schuster. Photographs copyright © 2001 by Cole Riggs Photography, Inc.

▼

Stewart, Tabori & Chang
(a company of La Martinière Groupe)
115 West 18th Street
New York, NY 10011
(800) 759-0190

■ **Home Cooking Around the World** *A Recipe Collection* by David Ricketts. Text copyright © 2001 by David Ricketts. Reprinted by permission of Stewart, Tabori & Chang, a company of La Martinière Groupe. Photographs copyright © 2001 by Mark Thomas.

■ **Napa Stories** *Profiles, Reflections & Recipes from the Napa Valley* by Michael Chiarello with Janet Fletcher. Text copyright © 2001 by NapaStyle, Inc. Reprinted by permission of Stewart, Tabori & Chang, a company of La Martinière Groupe. Photographs copyright © 2001 by Steven Rothfeld.

Ten Speed Press
P. O. Box 7123
Berkeley, CA 94707
(510) 559-1600
www.tenspeed.com

■ **Nuts** *Sweet and Savory Recipes from Diamond of California* by Tina Salter with Steve Siegelman. Text copyright © 2001 by Diamond of California. Reprinted by permission of Ten Speed Press. Food photography copyright © 2001 by Holly Stewart.

■ **Charlie Trotter's Meat & Game** by Charlie Trotter, with wine notes by Belinda Chang. Copyright © 2001 by Charlie Trotter. Reprinted by permission of Ten Speed Press. Food photographs © 2001 by Tim Turner.

■ **Soffritto** *Tradition and Innovation in Tuscan Cooking* by Benedetta Vitali. Text copyright © 2001 by Benedetta Vitali. Reprinted by permission of Ten Speed Press. Photographs copyright © 2001 by Cary Wolinsky.

268

■ **BayWolf Restaurant Cookbook** by Michael Wild and Lauren Lyle, with G. Earl Darny and Adele Novelli Crady. Copyright © 2001 by BayWolf Restaurant. Reprinted by permission of Ten Speed Press. Photographs by Laurie Smith.

Warner Books
(an AOL Time Warner company)
1271 Avenue of the Americas
New York, NY 10020
(800) 759-0190
www.twbookmark.com

■ **A Year in Chocolate** *Four Seasons of Unforgettable Desserts* by Alice Medrich. Copyright © 2001 by Alice Medrich. Reprinted by permission of Warner Books, Inc. Photographs by Michael Lamotte.

interior photo credits

Quentin Bacon PRIME TIME EMERIL 92

André Baranowski THE ELEMENTS OF TASTE 138

Kelly Bugden ONE POTATO, TWO POTATO 24, 140, 144, 157 (bottom), 180, 183 (bottom), 206, 232

Cole Riggs Photography FEARLESS BAKING 249

Beatriz Da Costa BAKER'S DOZEN COOKBOOK 209 (top and middle), 211, 216

Robert DiScalfani DA SILVANO COOKBOOK 194

Gus Fligate and Craig Robertson MADHUR JAFFREY'S STEP-BY-STEP COOKING 15 (bottom), 65, 67 (middle), 106–107, 109, 183 (top), 185, 191

Gentl & Hyers/Edge BOBBY FLAY COOKS AMERICAN 48, 67 (bottom), 74, 117 (bottom), 154

Michael Lamotte A YEAR IN CHOCOLATE 209 (bottom), 227, 251

David Loftus THE NAKED CHEF TAKES OFF 125, 157 (top), 173

Penina JOANNE WEIR'S MORE COOKING IN THE WINE COUNTRY 28, 177, 237, 239

Mai Pham PLEASURES OF THE VIETNAMESE TABLE 164, 203

Maria Robledo A NEW WAY TO COOK 117 (middle), 132 (top and bottom), 200

Steven Rothfeld NAPA STORIES 157 (middle), 167

Stuart Schwartz BIBA'S TASTE OF ITALY 117 (top), 151, 183 (middle), 188

Ellen Silverman ITALIAN HOLIDAY COOKING 113

Georgia Glynn Smith GORDON RAMSAY'S JUST DESSERTS 254

Laurie Smith BAYWOLF RESTAURANT COOKBOOK 15 (middle), 19, 59

Holly Stewart NUTS 15 (top), 17, 35, 257

Mark Thomas HOME COOKING AROUND THE WORLD 45

Tim Turner CHARLIE TROTTER'S MEAT & GAME 67 (top), 100

Cary Wolinsky SOFFRITTO 88, 115, 119, 197

Angela Wyant ENOTECA 63, 80, 94

jacket photo & illustration credits

Antonio Andreucci SOFFRITTO 13, 88, 114, 118, 174, 196, 204

Quentin Bacon PRIME TIME EMERIL 13, 90, 103, 148, 158

André Baranowski THE ELEMENTS OF TASTE 11, 71, 137

Kelly Bugden ONE POTATO, TWO POTATO 13, 23, 139, 143, 179, 205, 207, 231

Cole Riggs Photography FEARLESS BAKING 11, 213, 218, 242

Beatriz Da Costa (top right photo) PLEASURES OF THE VIETNAMESE TABLE 13, 163, 186, 202

BAKER'S DOZEN COOKBOOK 10, 210, 215, 223

Robert DiScalfani DA SILVANO COOKBOOK 11, 134, 193

Rupert Garcia BAYWOLF RESTAURANT COOKBOOK 10, 18, 32, 42, 58, 96

Gentl & Hyers/Edge BOBBY FLAY COOKS AMERICAN 10, 47, 73, 153

Robert Holmes (landscape photographs) NUTS 13, 16, 20, 34, 256

Michael Lamotte A YEAR IN CHOCOLATE 13, 226, 229, 250

David Loftus THE NAKED CHEF TAKES OFF 12, 124, 172

Duane Michals SECOND HELPINGS FROM UNION SQUARE CAFE 13, 50, 53, 60, 110, 120, 126, 160, 170

Melanie Parks LA BELLA CUCINA 10, 85, 130, 225

Mai Pham (bottom left photo) PLEASURES OF THE VIETNAMESE TABLE 13, 163, 186, 202

Steven Rothfeld NAPA STORIES 12, 166

Stuart Schwartz BIBA'S TASTE OF ITALY 10, 37, 128, 150, 187

Ellen Silverman ITALIAN HOLIDAY COOKING 12, 22, 56, 112

MADHUR JAFFREY'S STEP-BY-STEP COOKING 12, 64, 105, 184, 190

Georgia Glynn Smith GORDON RAMSAY'S JUST DESSERTS 11, 234, 253

Holly Stewart (food photographs) NUTS 13, 16, 20, 34, 256

Jeanne Strongin JOANNE WEIR'S MORE COOKING IN THE WINE COUNTRY 12, 27, 176, 236, 238

Mark Thomas HOME COOKING AROUND THE WORLD 12, 38, 44, 146

Michael Voltattorni CHARLIE TROTTER'S MEAT & GAME 11, 99

Angela Wyant ENOTECA 11, 62, 79, 82

photo & illustration credits

index

index

Index

body story

TEEN DREAMS

The Journey Through Puberty

BLACKBIRCH®
PRESS

THOMSON

GALE

San Diego • Detroit • New York • San Francisco • Cleveland • New Haven, Conn. • Waterville, Maine • London • Munich

LIBRARY OF CONGRESS CATALOGING-IN-PUBLICATION DATA

Teen dreams / Elaine Pascoe, book editor.
    p. cm. — (Body story)
Summary: Next-door neighbors Natalie and Darren discover the effects that gonadotrophins, testosterone, and estrogen have on their bodies and minds as they enter puberty.
Includes bibliographical references and index.
  ISBN 1-4103-0061-7 (hdbk. : alk. paper) — ISBN 1-4103-0182-6 (pbk. : alk. paper)
  1. Puberty—Juvenile literature. [1. Puberty. 2. Adolescence.] I. Pascoe, Elaine. II. Series.

  QP84.4.T44 2004
  612.6'61—dc21   2003009640

Eight-year-old neighbors Darren Bruff and Natalie Jack do not realize that their childhood days are numbered. Their purpose on this planet is to reproduce and pass on their genes. Right now, their immature bodies are not yet up to the task. But the process that will make it possible is about to begin.

For both boys and girls, puberty starts years before there are any outward signs—usually between the ages of eight and twelve. It is a rite of passage that will transform not just their bodies, but their minds as well. By the time Darren and Natalie are thirteen, they will be on a roller-coaster ride fueled by powerful body chemicals called hormones.

Puberty usually begins between the ages of eight and twelve.

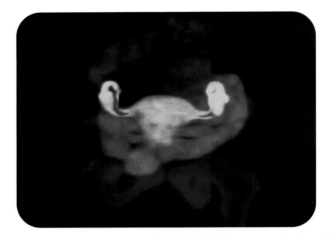

Deep in Natalie's abdomen are her ovaries. Inside her ovaries are half a million spherical cocoons, called follicles. Hidden within each follicle is an immature egg. For now, the eggs are in suspended animation.

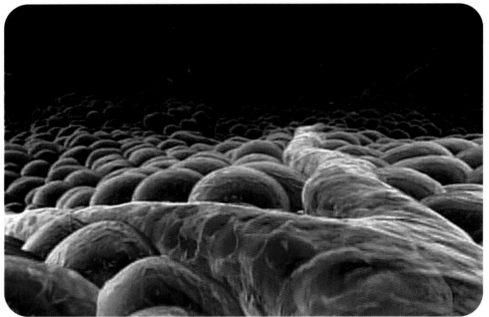

Top: Two ovaries (left and right) house the immature eggs.

Above: The follicles inside the ovaries are round cocoons.

In Darren's testicles nothing much is happening either. There are millions of cells, but no sign of sperm. The cells destined to create them lie dormant.

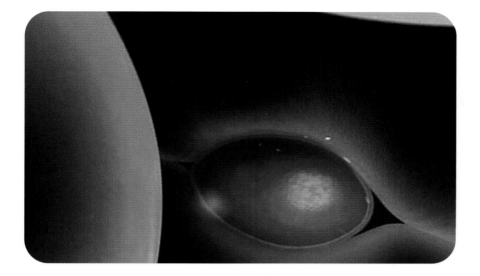

Natalie's and Darren's sex organs are waiting for a signal that will bring them to life and trigger puberty. No one knows why, but that signal always comes at night.

Top: In Darren's testicles, sperm cells lie dormant.

Above and left: Chemical signals that trigger puberty always occur at night.

5

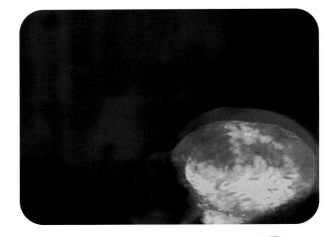

CHEMICAL MESSENGERS

Deep in Darren's brain a group of cells is activated. For the first time ever, the cells release chemical signals into the tiny blood vessels around them. Although the brain decides when puberty is to begin, it is these chemical messengers—hormones —that carry out the work.

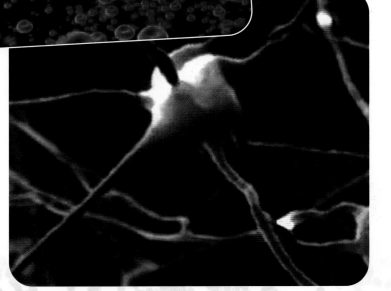

Top: A group of cells is activated deep inside the brain.

Middle: Hormones carrying chemical signals flow through the blood stream.

Bottom: Chemical signals are activated inside the brain, creating electrical circuits that relay messages.

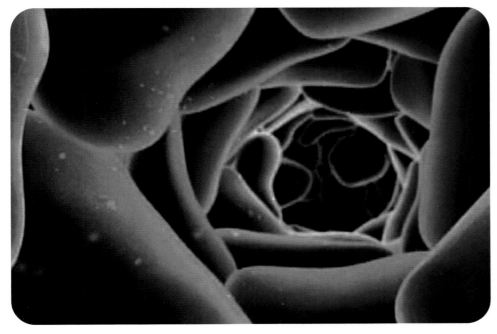

Now hormones known as gonadotropins fly through Darren's bloodstream. These chemical messengers carry signals from Darren's brain to the rest of his body. Night after night the hormones flood into his bloodstream— and begin to take effect. Inside his testicles, cells begin to divide. They organize themselves into tubes, building factories that will one day produce sperm.

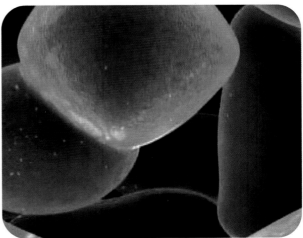

Top: The cells organize into tubes that will one day house sperm production.

Above: Inside the testicles, cells begin to divide

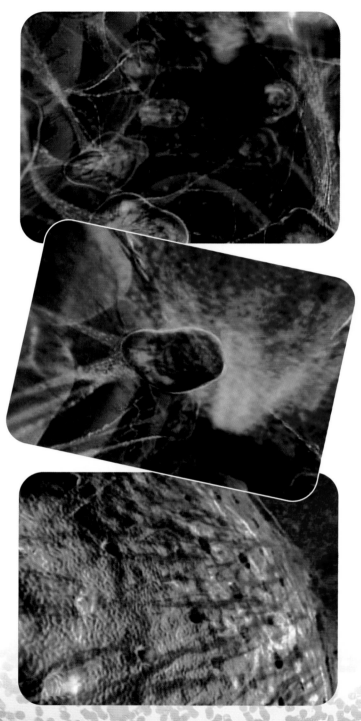

As the years pass, Darren's brain steps up the pace. The signal gets stronger, and the changes taking place in Darren's testicles occur faster and faster. Between the newly grown tubes, gonadotropins seep out and soak into specialist cells—triggering them to produce the male sex hormone, testosterone.

By the time Darren is thirteen, he has amassed enough testosterone for his body to begin transforming into the body of a man.

Top and middle: Gonadotropins seep out between the newly grown tubes.

Bottom: The hormone testosterone is produced by specialist cells.

The changes in Darren mean he will soon be able to reproduce. But to be a mature adult, he also has to want to reproduce. Inside his brain, testosterone seeps from blood vessels into the fluid that surrounds his brain cells. Soon it will transform his mind.

Above: At the age of thirteen, a boy has usually amassed enough testosterone for his body to transform into that of a man.

Below: Testosterone has a powerful effect on the brain.

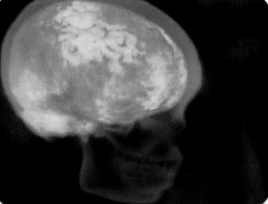

Left and below: Testosterone "wakes up" brain cells that form connections for desiring sex.

The testosterone that that floods through Darren's brain begins to soak through the membranes of dormant cells, triggering a chemical reaction. The testosterone brings to life a group of interconnected brain cells. This is Darren's reproductive circuit. It will give him the desire for sex.

Darren gets a clear sign that this desire has sprung to life when he shows up for band practice one day and finds rehearsals in progress for a school play —a hip-hop version of *Romeo and Juliet*. Natalie is trying out for the part of Juliet. Watching her read, Darren suddenly finds that the girl next door has become the woman of his dreams.

Top, middle, bottom: Testosterone in Darren's brain has transformed the way he thinks—and how his body reacts.

NEW EMOTIONS

Over the past five years Natalie's brain has been just as active as Darren's has. But while gonadotropins transform his testicles, they bring to life her ovaries. Inside the ovaries, the hormone has stimulated a few of the follicles to grow, so that the eggs concealed inside them begin to mature. As the follicle wall grows and swells, a new hormone seeps out—the female sex hormone, estrogen. It flows out of the follicles into her blood.

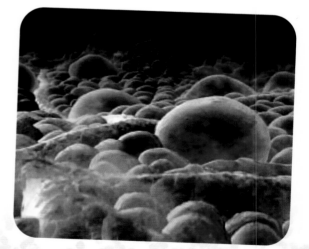

Right: Gonadoptropins in Natalie's ovaries have brought the round follicles to life.

Estrogen will drive Natalie's transformation into a sexually mature woman. It also makes permanent changes in her brain, bringing to life inactive areas. This is probably because the hormones stimulate nerve endings, encouraging them to form new connections.

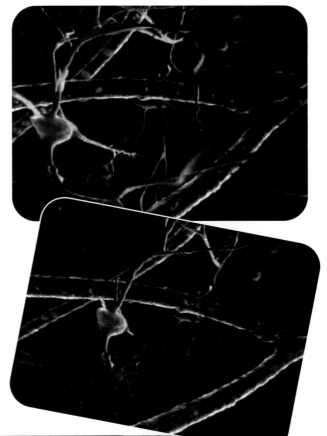

Top, middle, bottom: The hormone estrogen stimulates the previously dormant brain cells in Natalie's brain and causes her to start thinking about sex.

These new circuits fire powerful new emotions. And sometimes those feelings erupt in family confrontations like this:

Natalie: I'm getting a tattoo.

Mr. and Mrs. Jackson: You are not.

Natalie: Oh, I might have known.

Mr. Jackson: Known what?

Natalie: You automatically say no. No, no, no, no. Are you programmed to say no? You never let me do what I want. You're so predictable. I don't even know why you had me in the first place!

Natalie's feelings are suddenly much stronger, but she has not yet learned how to control them.

Top, middle, bottom: Surging hormones cause powerful changes in the brain—changes that are often strange and overwhelming.

HORMONES

Whether you are a boy or a girl, your body produces testosterone and estrogen. It also produces other sexual hormones, including luteinizing hormone (LH for short), and follicle-stimulating hormone (FSH for short). Depending on whether you are a guy or a girl, these hormones go to work on different parts of your body during puberty.

In the male body, LH and FSH travel through the blood and give the testicles the signal to begin the production of testosterone and sperm. Testosterone is the hormone that causes most of the changes in a guy's body during puberty. Sperm cells must be produced in order for males to reproduce.

In girls, FSH and LH target the ovaries, which contain eggs that have been in the ovaries since birth. The hormones stimulate the ovaries to begin producing another hormone called estrogen. Estrogen, along with FSH and LH, prepares a girl's body for pregnancy.

Even though estrogen is thought of as primarily a woman's hormone, it is actually critical in the male body as well. Without estrogen, sperm are ineffective. That means, without estrogen, a man is infertile. In 1997, researchers concluded that estrogen was vital for fluid reabsorption during the transfer of sperm in fluid from the testes through the efferent ductules to the epididymis, where sperm matures and is stored. Efferent ductules are small tubes that produce concentrated semen. Without the estrogen, excess fluid dilutes the sperm and makes the male infertile.

Testosterone is considered the "male" hormone, but female bodies also produce it. Testosterone is produced by the adrenal glands in both males and females and, in small amounts, by the ovaries in females. In women, testosterone is converted to estrogen, the main female sex hormone.

While Natalie must learn to live with estrogen, Darren is in the grip of testosterone. He is trying to cope with a brain that wants sex. When Natalie begins a casual chat, his reproductive circuit interferes with his ability to hold a conversation—leaving him tongue-tied.

As in all men, Darren's hormone levels soar at night. As testosterone rises, his reproductive circuit goes into overdrive and even takes control of his dreams.

Right and below: Darren's testosterone levels have gotten high enough that even his dreams are now about sex.

But there is more to testosterone than creating a sex drive. Testosterone also makes Darren more competitive and assertive—attributes that will help him get sex. With his new assertiveness, he decides to try out for the play himself. Thanks to his clear singing voice—which has not yet broken, or deepened in pitch—he lands the role of Romeo, playing opposite Natalie's Juliet.

Top and bottom: Testosterone enhances certain other sexually related behaviors, such as aggression, competitiveness, and anger.

GROWTH SPURTS

Natalie started puberty later than Darren did, but she is growing much faster than him and looks more mature—all thanks to estrogen. When estrogen in her body reached a critical level, it triggered a growth spurt, and since then special plates in her bones have been growing rapidly.

Right and below: In women, estrogen triggers bone growth, which occurs rapidly during puberty.

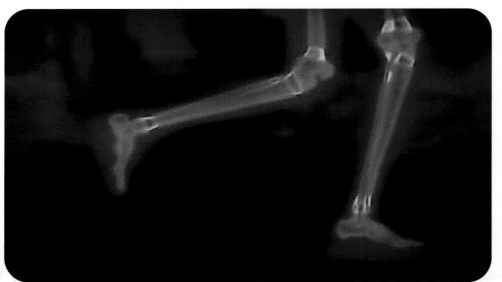

To catch up with her, Darren will need his own supply of estrogen. His brain has a remarkable way to manufacture the hormone: It converts excess testosterone into estrogen.

But Darren will have to wait for his growth spurt. Testosterone levels build up gradually in boys' bodies to the point where there is excess testosterone to convert. This is why boys seem to mature more slowly than girls, and why girls often find older boys, who appear as sexually mature as themselves, more attractive.

Top: When Darren's body has built up enough testosterone, his brain will help to convert excess testosterone into estrogen.

Right: Girls often find older boys more attractive.

Just as Darren needs estrogen, Natalie needs the male sex hormone testosterone. In fact, both sexes need both hormones, though in different quantities. Men have approximately ten times more testosterone than women do, and women have around ten times more estrogen than men do.

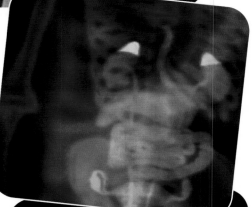

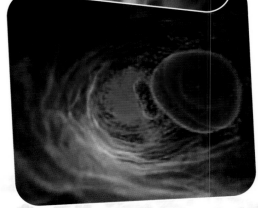

Middle: The adrenal glands on top of Natalie's kidneys pump testosterone into her blood.
Bottom: The blood carries testosterone to the brain, where it stimulates the sex drive.

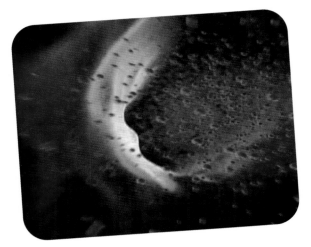

Left and below: As testosterone floods the brain, sexual attraction intensifies.

Natalie's adrenal glands, which sit on top of her kidneys, pump small amounts of testosterone into her blood. Her blood carries it to her brain, where it stimulates her reproductive circuit and gives her the sex drive she needs to pass on her genes. Now, when her good-looking classmate David Blane asks her out, she is interested.

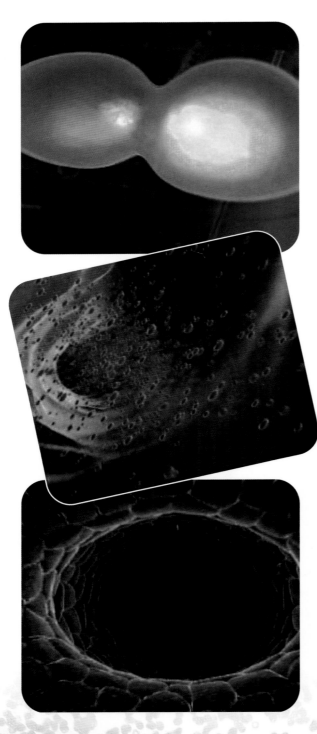

CHANGES SEEN AND UNSEEN

Darren does not know it, but changes inside his testicles are bringing him closer to furthering his genes. Deep within the wall of a tube, a dormant cell is coming to life. The cell divides. The new cell that is formed will become Darren's very first sperm.

Meanwhile, Darren and Natalie are both losing control of their bodies to hormones. The levels of testosterone and estrogen in their blood are rising with every passing day, slowly transforming their bodies to prepare them for sex.

Top: When the first cell inside the testicles divides, it is the beginning of the first sperm.

Middle: Testosterone levels in the blood continue to increase.

Bottom: The hormones in both bodies transform them physically.

One of the main objectives of sex hormones is to trigger changes that will make people more attractive to potential mates. But sometimes the effect is just the opposite. Testosterone sets off a reaction inside tiny glands, called sebaceous glands, in the skin. The glands produce an oily substance called sebum that normally flows up onto the skin. But as Darren's testosterone levels surge, his glands produce so much sebum that it clogs his pores. It becomes a breeding ground for bacteria, which infect the pores. Sebum gave our ape ancestors glossy coats, making them attractive to other apes. All it gives Darren is acne.

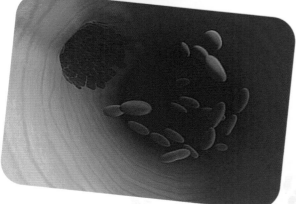

An oily substance called sebum is triggered by high testosterone levels. When an excess of sebum is produced, it clogs pores in the skin and causes pimples.

Darren's body is overreacting to escalating hormone levels, and acne is not the only result. Testosterone has made his genitals so sensitive that even the slightest touch can trigger a response. This reaction is a reflex; his brain is not involved. Darren's penis seems to have a mind of its own. In fact, it is quite common for teenage boys to have as many as twenty reflex erections a day.

Gradually Darren's body will adjust to higher levels of testosterone, sparing him this embarrassment most of the time.

Left and below: Testosterone makes genitals very sensitive. Even the slightest touch can trigger an uncontrollable reaction.

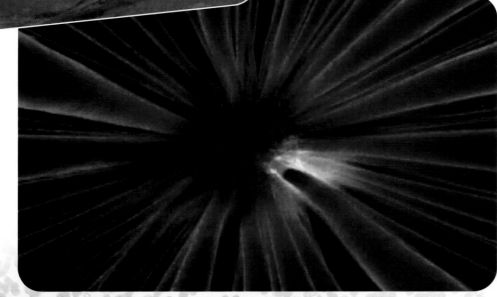

ESTROGEN'S EFFECTS

Natalie is luckier. While Darren suffers at the hand of hormones, she is benefiting. She produces sebum, but estrogen keeps the levels down, reducing the effects on her skin for now.

Estrogen is having other effects. Until recently there were few visible differences between her body and a boy's. But sex hormones are now sculpting her body into a different shape—designed to be attractive to men.

Top and above: In females, estrogen triggers body changes that create a new shape.

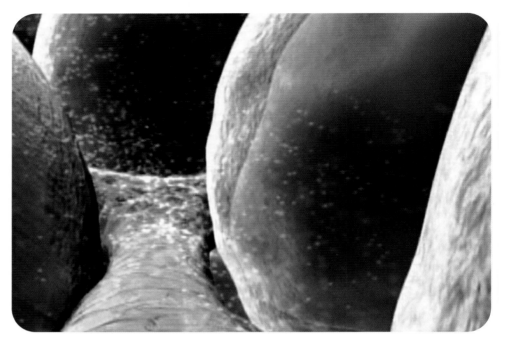

Under the influence of estrogen, fat cells in Natalie's chest draw fat globules from her bloodstream. As the fat cells swell, her breasts begin to grow. The same things are happening to the fat cells on her hips and buttocks, giving Natalie the beginnings of an "hourglass" shape.

Top: Fat cells from the blood are drawn to specific areas of the body, such as breasts, hips, and buttocks.

Above: As fat cells enlarge specific areas of the female body, a girl begins to look like a woman.

Natalie thinks she is more mature than Darren is, but her body is no closer than his to being able to reproduce. In her ovary, her enlarged follicles continue to grow, but they need to swell to one hundred times their present size before the eggs contained within them can reach maturity.

Left and below: The changes brought on by puberty are dramatic—both physically and emotionally. Bodies become more mature and new sexual energy causes pent up emotions that need to be released.

TESTOSTERONE'S TRICKS

So far testosterone has been nothing but trouble for Darren. But now he finally has enough for his brain to convert excess into estrogen, triggering his growth spurt. His skeleton is lengthening at a rate of 1 centimeter a month, faster than any time since he was a baby.

Right and below: When estrogen triggers bone growth, the changes are quick and dramatic.

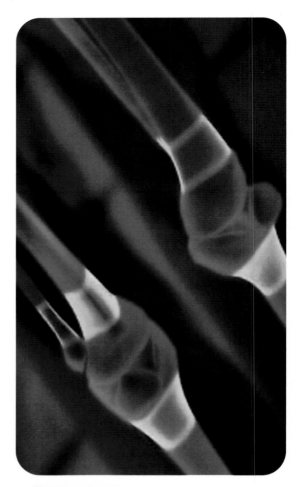

Below: A growing and changing body creates challenges for the brain as it adjusts to larger and longer limbs.

Being taller will help make Darren more attractive to girls, but in the short term such rapid growth has its drawbacks. He becomes clumsy. As Darren moves around, his brain must track exactly where every part of his body is, to keep his movements coordinated. But as his limbs grow, his brain must adjust. And because his legs are growing so quickly, his brain just cannot keep up with the changes.

Darren's hormones are working to make him more and more sexually attractive. His muscles are made up of fibrous strands. Testosterone makes these fibers multiply, causing the muscles to thicken and bulking up his biceps. But the fastest-multiplying cells in Darren's body are in his penis. If the rest of Darren grew as much during puberty, he would soon be over 9 feet tall.

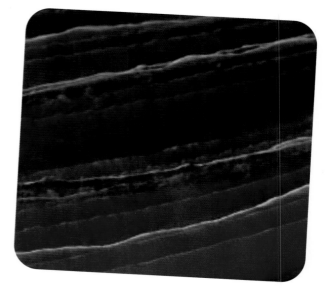

Above: Muscles are made of fiberous strands.

Below: Testosterone causes the muscle strands to thicken and become larger and stronger.

Darren's rising testosterone levels have another effect: increased aggression. A snide remark from David Blane now makes him fighting mad—he sees David as a rival. For our distant ancestors, fighting for a mate was a necessary skill for the sexually mature male. In fact, men's brains are wired up so that circuits for aggression and sex overlap.

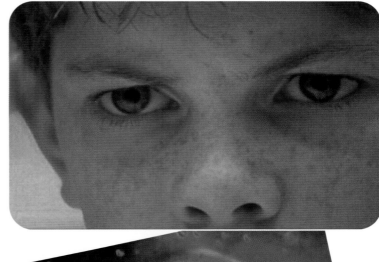

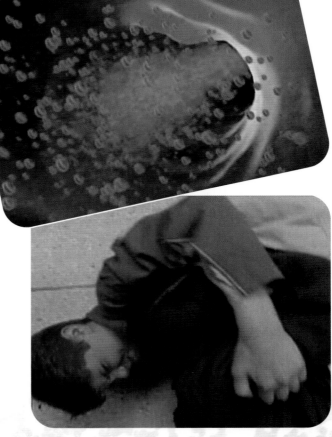

Top: High aggression levels are caused by testosterone.

Middle: As testosterone flows through the blood to the brain, aggression increases. The final result *(below)* can often be physical conflict.

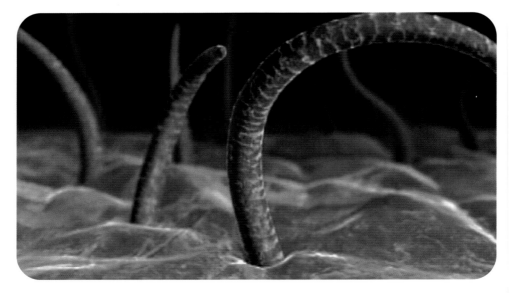

Testosterone also has effects on Natalie. It causes hair to grow at her groin and armpits and contributes to body odor, which is another outward sign of Natalie's emerging sexual maturity. Our ancestors found it attractive. But in our hygiene-conscious world, body odor tends to have the opposite effect.

Top: Hair follicles are stimulated by testosterone.

Middle: During puberty, hair grows in armpits, the groin, and other areas.

Bottom: Eventually, Darren will begin to grow hair on his face.

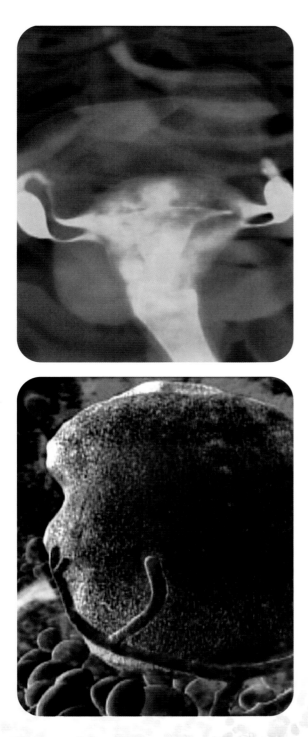

A MILESTONE

All the changes in Natalie's body are designed to aid a process still unfolding in her ovaries. There gonadotropins have caused one follicle to grow so large that the egg concealed inside it is almost mature. This one follicle is now producing three-fourths of all the estrogen in her body. But there is a problem. The bigger the follicle grows, the more gonadotropins it needs to survive —and Natalie's brain can not yet manufacture enough. Starved of the hormones it needs, the follicle starts to die, killing the egg inside it. It stops producing estrogen, causing the levels of that hormone in Natalie's body to plummet.

Top: The gonadotropins in the female ovaries cause the egg follicles to grow larger.

Bottom: When estrogen levels are high enough, the eggs inside the follicles will grow to maturity.

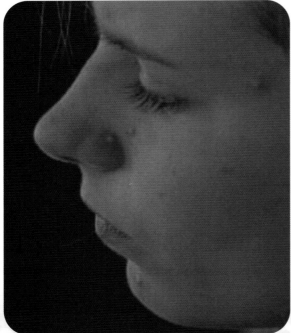

It does not take long for the results to show. Within two days there is no longer enough estrogen in Natalie's skin to keep sebum production down. It is Natalie's turn to get pimples.

Top and left: As estrogen levels fall, sebum production increases and causes pimples.

The shortage of estrogen has even more drastic effects beneath her skin. Inside her womb, layers of cells form a lining designed to sustain a growing fetus; but without estrogen, the blood vessels that feed these cells are cut off. The womb lining dies. Layer by layer, the cells begin to shear off. Natalie is having her first period; she has begun to menstruate.

Top: Without sustained estrogen, the cells inside the womb will die and be shed from the body, causing menstruation.

Below: Blood vessels that feed the womb cells are cut off without estrogen.

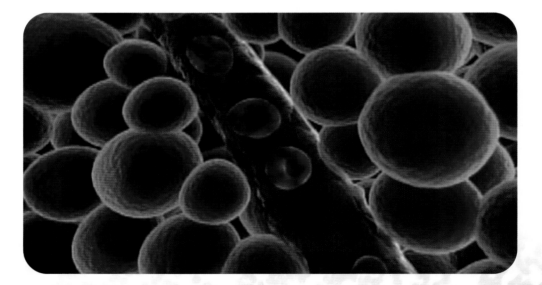

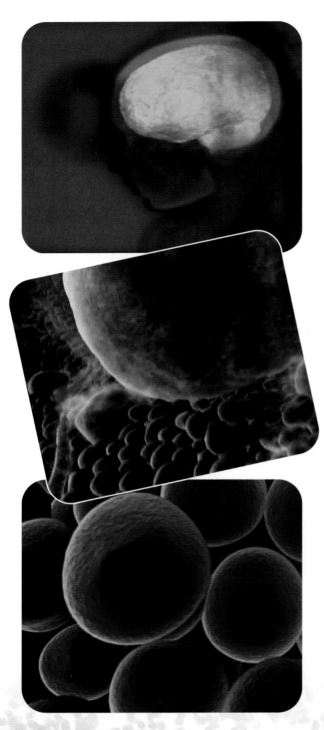

This first period is unique because it has not been triggered by the creation of a fertile egg. It is a major milestone of puberty, but Natalie is still incapable of reproduction. Still, at the age of thirteen Natalie's body is locked into a monthly cycle by her brain. Her brain cells drive the release of gonadotropins. Once again, in her ovaries, the hormone stimulates follicles to grow— with one growing larger than any other. The follicles produce estrogen, which triggers the cells lining her uterus to multiply.

Top: By age 13, the brain will begin to coordinate the monthly cycle that stimulates hormone production with the intent of bringing an egg inside her ovaries to maturity.

Middle: Gonadotropins stimulate egg follicle growth.

Bottom: A growing follicle triggers the cells in the uterus to multiply.

In the space of ten days, her womb lining has completely regrown.

For some women, the start of menstruation brings some unwelcome side effects. These include stomach cramps, back pain, and moodiness triggered by hormonal changes. But not all women experience these problems to the same degree.

Top, middle, bottom: For many women, menstruation brings moodiness, cramps, and back pain.

PRODUCTION LINES

Next door, Darren is about to experience a less visible, but equally dramatic change. Sperm production lines have begun throughout his testicles. As new cells are made, they are shunted up against the walls of the tubes.

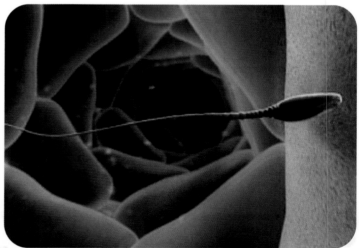

Top: A sperm cell is about to break through the wall of the testicles.

Bottom: A fully formed sperm begins its journey to a storage chamber.

Now a remarkable transformation begins. One of the cells divides, forming Darren's first sperm. Too small to be seen with the naked eye, the sperm cells are shaped like tiny tadpoles. Darren's genes are packed into the head, while the rest of the cell is a threadlike tail that is designed to act as a propeller.

As the production line picks up pace, sperm collect in a chamber, ready and waiting to fertilize an egg. But it will still be another five years before Darren's sperm factories work at full adult capacity, churning out one thousand sperm every second.

Top, middle, bottom: Sperm are carried to the storage chamber by contractions in the tubes inside the testicles.

Meanwhile, the night of the play has arrived, and testosterone has just one last cruel trick to play on Darren. The levels of the hormone in his blood are now high enough to trigger the cells in his vocal cords to multiply. His vocal cords are having their own growth spurt.

This page: As Darren sings a song from the show, his voice begins to "crack." The cracking is the result of lengthening vocal cords.

As Darren's vocal cords get longer, his voice will get deeper. But just as he has had difficulty controlling his fast-growing arms and legs, it is becoming difficult for Darren's brain to properly control his vocal cords now that they are changing. He manages to sing and say his lines, but with his voice breaking uncontrollably, he can hardly trust himself to speak at all.

Top, middle, bottom:
Testosterone has caused the vocal cords to lengthen, which deepens the voice. As this happens, the voice can change from high to low uncontrollably.

FINAL STEPS

Darren and Natalie are now almost capable of reproduction. Their sex organs have only one small step to take.

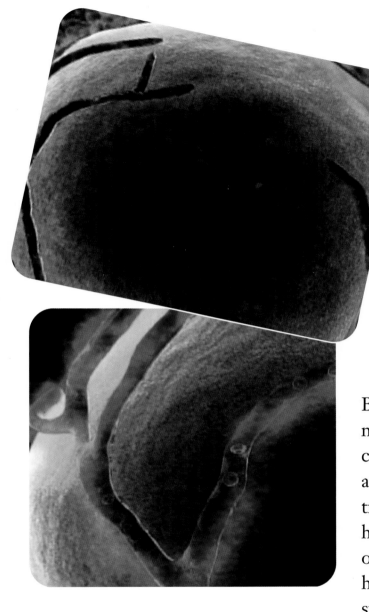

While Darren's testicles make millions of sperm, Natalie's ovaries have concentrated on producing just one perfect egg. This time the enlarged follicle is doing everything in its power to stay alive until the egg concealed inside reaches maturity. Blood vessels bring extra nourishment. As it reaches a critical size, the follicle sends a signal to Natalie's brain, triggering a massive surge of hormones—the biggest pulse of gonadotropins her body has ever experienced. The surge reaches the egg inside the follicle, finally stimulating it to mature.

Top and above: As the egg follicle matures, it sends stronger signals to the brain, which trigger large surges of gonadotropins.

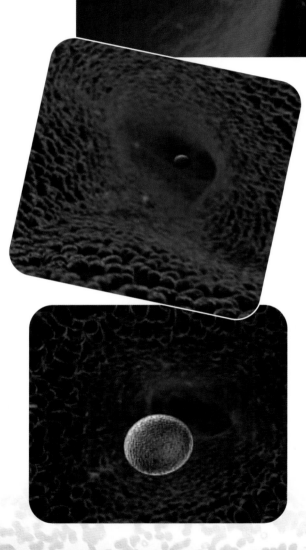

Now her body is ready to release her first mature egg. The egg bursts out of its follicle, out of the ovary, and down one of her fallopian tubes toward her womb. In two weeks time this egg will be swept away in another period. But it is just the first of nearly five hundred eggs that Natalie will produce during her lifetime, one every month for about forty years.

Top: The mature egg bursts out of its follicle.

Middle: The egg begins a journey through a fallopian tube.

Bottom: The fallopian tube will eventually deposit the egg in the womb.

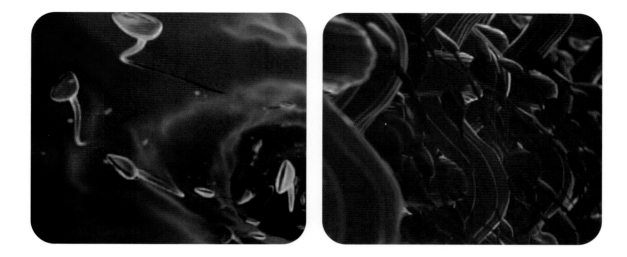

Meanwhile, Darren is about to find out that he has reached sexual maturity. Signals from his reproductive circuit tell the chamber that holds his sperm to contract. For the first time, Darren's genes are set free into the world.

Top: As sperm builds in the storage chamber, the chamber becomes filled. When the chamber contains enough sperm, brain signals will tell the chamber to involuntarily eject the sperm.

Although they have reached these milestones, Darren and Natalie still do not have the bodies or the minds of mature adults. They are still learning to deal with all the changes that are taking place. Eventually, they will both feel more in control of their bodies and their emotions. At that point, they will be able to function as fully mature and responsible adults.

Puberty is a long and complicated process. When it is over, the body and the mind are both ready to support the responsible behavior of mature adults.

GLOSSARY

adrenal glands Organs on top of the kidneys that produce hormones.

estradiol A female sex hormone.

estrogen A female sex hormone.

follicles The parts of the ovary that contain developing eggs.

gonadotropins Hormones that stimulate the ovaries and testicles.

hormones Naturally occurring substances in the body that affect cells.

menstruation The discharge of blood and tissue debris from the uterus.

ovaries The organs in females that produce eggs and sex hormones.

puberty The period during which boys and girls reach sexual maturity.

sebaceous glands Glands that produce an oily substance called sebum.

sperm The male reproductive cells that fertilize eggs.

testicles Male reproductive glands that produce sperm.

testosterone The male sex hormone.

uterus The organ in female mammals in which a fertilized egg develops.

INDEX